GW00985833

the modern japanese tea room

the modern japanese tea room

Michael Freeman

DAMIANI

DAMIANI©2007

DAMIANI Editore
Via Zanardi, 376
Tel. +39.051.6350805
Fax +39.051.6347188
40131 Bologna - Italy
www.damianieditore.com
info@damianieditore.it

Printed on
Magno Satin 170 gr.
distributed by

Text and design © 2007 Eight Books Limited
Photographs © 2007 Michael Freeman

All rights reserved, No part of this publication may be reproduced or transmitted in any form or by any means, electronic or mechanical, including photocopying, recording or by any information storage or retrieval system, without prior permission in writing from the publisher.

ISBN 978 88 89431 87 0

Printed in Italy by Grafiche Damiani srl, Bologna

Contents

"The Way of Tea is naught but this:
first you boil water,
then you make the tea and drink it." *Sen no Rikyu (1522–1591)*

Introduction

This is a book about a series of experiments, undertaken individually and with little in the way of publicity, by contemporary Japanese architects and designers. The site for the experiments is the most Japanese of spaces, the tea-ceremony room, or *chashitsu*. To appreciate just how radical is the idea of creating new and imaginative versions of this small, traditional room, we first need a background in the tea ceremony itself, because this is a very loaded space — charged with a six hundred-year history of philosophy, religion, art, social intercourse, and Japanese-ness. Its great attraction for architects and designers as noted as Arata Isozaki, Kengo Kuma, and Shigeru Uchida, among many others, is evidence of how seriously it is still taken.

The sparse interior of a portable *chashitsu*, made of woven bamboo strips stained black, the latest in a series of similar structures by designer Shigeru Uchida.

The *teishu*, or host, at a seated tea ceremony (*ryureiseki*) in a modern setting in Nishi-Azabu, Tokyo, with backlit screens of calligraphy. She is holding a *fukusa*, a silk cloth that is used in the ritual cleaning of the tea equipment as well as for holding hot lids.

The tea ceremony, which exists only in Japanese culture, is certainly an occasion on which tea is prepared, offered and drunk, but ideologically it is much more than that. The duality of the simple yet profound lies at the heart of *chanoyu*, or the Way of Tea, and accounts for many of the apparent contradictions and ambiguities in the way it is described and explained. A list of short explanations offered over the years by those closely involved in the Way of Tea, in increasing order of ambiguity, can shed some light on this concept:

"... a ritualised form of serving tea, expressing 'Wakeiseijaku' — or mutual respect and thoughtfulness, which brings harmony among and between people and things — by appreciating art pieces that are presented during the ceremony." *Enshu School of Tea*

"The tea ceremony requires years of training and practice ... yet the whole of this art, as to its detail, signifies no more than the making and serving of a cup of tea. The supremely important matter is that the act be performed in the most perfect, most polite, most graceful, most charming manner possible." *Lafcadio Hearn (1850–1904)*

"... a cult founded on the adoration of the beautiful among the sordid facts of everyday existence. It inculcates purity and harmony, the mystery of mutual charity, the romanticism of the social order. It is essentially a worship of the Imperfect, as it is a tender attempt to accomplish something possible in this impossible thing we know as life." *Kakuzo Okakura (1863–1919)*, The Book of Tea

"Tea is not a game and not an art; one taste of tea refreshes and purifies and gives enlightenment to the universal law." *Murata Shuko (1423–1502)*

"Tea with us became more than an idealisation of the form of drinking; it is a religion of the art of life." *Kakuzo Okakura (1863–1919)*, The Book of Tea

"The Way of Tea is naught but this: first you boil water, then you make the tea and drink it." *Sen no Rikyu (1522-1591)*

These quotations, some seemingly in opposition, give a necessary glimpse of the complexity of the tea ceremony, as it is so inadequately described in English. It evades precise definition, even in Japanese.

Preparations behind the scenes
at Gogoku-ji Temple, Tokyo,
during a special day of
successive tea ceremonies.

In particular, the terminology does not translate adequately, and even the basic concept of the space in which the tea ceremony takes place — the subject of this book — cannot be conveyed in English without drawing in unwanted connotations. So here first is a brief history, in an attempt to answer the obvious questions: why tea? why a ceremony? and why so profoundly linked to art, ideology, and religion?

Tea originated in China, probably in Yunnan, and achieved great popularity during the Tang Dynasty (618–907). There are a great many varieties, but the three basic types, which depend on the manufacture and in particular on the amount of fermentation allowed. These are black tea, *oolong* tea, and green tea. Black tea, the type most commonly drunk in the West, is made by allowing the harvested leaves to ferment fully. If the leaves are left to lose some of their moisture for a short while, and then heated, they become half-fermented, or *oolong*, tea. Green tea is unfermented, made by heating the leaves immediately they are picked. A further refinement of cultivation is needed to make the powdered green tea, or *matcha*, which is used in the tea ceremony: covers are put over the tea plants as soon as the buds appear to shield them from direct sunlight, and this causes the plants to produce more chlorophyll and large, sweet leaves. The veins and stalks are then removed before grinding the leaves to a powder.

The appeal of tea, based largely on its caffeine content and the protein theanine which is mainly responsible for its flavour, spread internationally, first within Asia at the time of the Tang Dynasty, then later, from the sixteenth century with the beginnings of international maritime trade. The eighth-century *Cha Jing* (The Classic of Tea) written by Lu Yu between 733 and 804 was the first book to make a systematic description of tea drinking, including its history, utensils, and the sense of a philosophy of moderation and frugality. So it was that by the eighth century tea was beginning to acquire an ideological context. The techniques, materials, and utensils were studied, a new range of skills was becoming recognised, and in this context it was inevitable that the *occasion* of preparing and drinking tea also began to be seen as somewhat special. To a greater or lesser degree, tea drinking acquired ceremony.

If it seems at first a little unusual that such a commonplace beverage should inspire ritual, it is worth remembering that even in Britain tea gained its own cultural trappings, although hardly so deep as in

Japan. Black tea (as opposed to the fresh green tea used in the Japanese ceremony) became a favoured drink by the middle of the eighteenth century. Afternoon tea, said to have originated with the Duchess of Bedford in the early 1800s, became an institution. It is interesting to view it from the Japanese perspective. From the Omotesenke School (one of the tea-ceremony schools) comes this description: "The tea-loving British created a unique culture of black tea. The custom known as afternoon tea also means a light meal taken between lunch and a late dinner. It is a British custom to enjoy a short conversation while eating scones and whipped cream or sandwiches with a pot of tea. People drink it with milk or sugar, according to taste, and there is also the American style of drinking it with lemon."

Yet it was in Japan that tea drinking became a ceremony of importance, with connections to philosophy, religion, and even politics. The first records of tea in Japan date to the ninth century, during the period of influence of the Tang Dynasty in China. However, relationships between the two countries faded, and tea drinking did not immediately take root. This happened three centuries later, when during the Southern Song Dynasty a Japanese monk, Eisai, went to Zhejiang in 1168 to study Zen Buddhism. He returned to Japan in 1193, taking a tea plant, and wrote the first Japanese book on tea, *Kissa Yojoki* (Drinking Tea for Health). A friend of Eisai, Moyo-e, also promoted the drinking of powdered tea leaves as an aid to well-being and longevity, as well as an ascetic aid to Zen training. Tea became inseparably connected to Zen and its importance was assured. In particular, it became apart from the common world, similar to Buddhist religious training, and acquired the sense of metaphor for a detached and pure way of life. The priest Dairin Soto proclaimed "*chazen ichimi*", "tea and Zen are one and the same".

Nevertheless, as tea drinking was embraced by the *daimyo*, or feudal lords, it became more elaborate. There was a type of gathering known as *tocha*, in which prizes were awarded for guessing the origin of particular teas, and during the fifteenth century there developed a tea banquet known as *chakai*, at which works of art were displayed, and fine utensils imported from China (*karamono*). Connoisseurs of these things, known as *dobishu*, acquired a certain status, advising the Shogun and nobility.

To the left is a black lacquer *natsume*, containing tea powder. To the right a tea-ceremony bowl (*chawan*) with bamboo scoop (*chashaku*) and bamboo whisk (*chasen*).

The reaction to this, which set the path for the Way of Tea that has continued until now, occurred in the late fifteenth and early sixteenth centuries. It began with the Zen priest Murata Shuko (1423–1502), who re-united tea with spirituality and simplicity, and brought it to the common people. Instead of splendour, he sought restraint and a form of muted beauty. His ideas were continued by Takeno Joo (1502–1555) and developed to their full expression by Sen no Rikyu (1522–1591). Rikyu became tea master to Shogun Hideyoshi, the man who unified Japan for the first time in history. His aim was to create a Way of Tea that was focused on an intense spiritual exchange between people.

Central to this revolution (as it certainly was, promoting humility and the ordinary over the high elaborate style of the courts), were two concepts that to this day remain elusive in definition, *wabi* and *sabi*. *Wabi* derives from the verb *wabu*, meaning "dejection, bitterness, being reduced to poverty". *Sabi* is derived from *sabu*, meaning "to get old, to be discoloured". The point of fascination here is that these essentially negative emotions were converted into terms expressing a very particular kind of beauty — an aesthetic of ascetism. *Wabi* has come to mean humble and simple, while *sabi* means rusted and weathered, and the two combined in the expression *wabi-sabi*, suggest what the Zen scholar Daisetz T. Suzuki termed "an active aesthetical appreciation of poverty." The tea-ceremony room and its utensils are the most lasting and visible expression of these tea ideals, and it was Sen no Rikyu who is credited with their final traditional form. He was able to reduce the size to the minimum of two tatami mats — an expression of *wabi* — and to choose and commission utensils in a similarly "impoverished" style.

The exact nuances of *wabi-sabi* continue to be debated. Architect Kisho Kurokawa, whose tea garden appears on pages 154–159, disputes what he sees as the prevalence of a too-narrow interpretation of *wabi*, to the point of actually inventing a term, *hanasuki*, to replace the normal *wabisuki* (simple taste). "Traditionally," he writes, "*wabi* has been thought of as silence as opposed to loquacity; darkness as opposed to light; simplicity as opposed to complexity; spareness as opposed to decoration; monochrome as opposed to colour; the grass hut, not the aristocrat's mansion. Even in school texts, *wabi* is defined as

13

A type of *wagashi*, or sweet soft cake, known as *joyo manju*. *Wagashi* can be eaten either with thin tea, as shown here, or with thick tea, known as *koicha*.

Higashi, or dry sweets, that are normally served during a tea ceremony with thin tea, or *usucha*.

an aesthetic of nothingness." Kurokawa argues that the true meaning is a co-existence of the gorgeous and the plain, and without knowing the former one cannot appreciate the latter. Those who do not first know the loveliness of blossoms can never live in a plain thatched hut. "It is an aesthetic of double code, in which we are asked to gaze at the roughly thatched hut while recalling the gorgeous flowers and leaves. It is an ambiguous, symbiotic aesthetic, which simultaneously embraces splendour and simplicity."

There is also a special concept in Japanese called *mitate*, akin to substitution. In the context of the tea ceremony it refers to the use of objects in something other than the form for which they were intended. One of Sen no Rikyu's inspirations was to take discarded and everyday, common objects and re-use them, so transforming their meaning and value. One example was a gourd that had been a water flask, converted to holding a flower in the *tokonoma*. This was one of the ways in which the veneration of elaborate Chinese utensils was challenged, and has remained to the present.

Another key concept is *ichigo ichie*, which means literally "one encounter in a lifetime". The occasion on which the host and guest meet is, in other words, unique. There is no way of knowing if it will ever happen again, and the moment should be treasured as once in a lifetime. There is only this single opportunity for the host to make tea for the guest, and so it demands the greatest effort. This is the essence of hospitality that plays such an important role. I appreciated this for the first time when arriving to photograph the private tea-ceremony room of architect Atsushi Kitagawara (pages 40–43). It had never been photographed, despite having been built eight years before, so this was already a privilege. Realising that I had little experience of the tea ceremony, Kitagawara and his wife thought it would be interesting for me to have one in relaxed circumstances. Instead of a normally prescribed scroll painting, he had displayed a photographic print, the work of a friend of his. It was this gesture of thoughtfulness that made me realise that preparation and consideration were very much a part of the occasion.

The purpose of a *chaji*, or full tea ceremony, is to allow the host an opportunity to express the utmost hospitality to his or her guests. The *chashitsu* and its approach garden should provide the optimum

A modern preparation area for tea ceremonies (*mizuya*) at Kikyo-ya, a shop specialising in selling confections (*wagashi*) in Nagoya.

physical and spiritual setting for expressing this hospitality. Guests take the path, walking along the stepping stones, stopping at the *tsukubai*, or water basin, where they wash hands and mouth in a ritual of purification. At the entrance to the *chashitsu* they remove their shoes and enter, one at a time, through a doorway so small that they must crouch and crawl. A *chaji*, the full tea ceremony, can take about four hours, and has two "acts", in which each person plays a ritual part. In the first "act", or *shoza*, the guests receive a light meal, or *kaiseki*, and the host prepares the charcoal in the brazier. The guests then retire to the garden for a short while. The host then calls them back for the second "act", or *goza*. During this, the host prepares and offers two servings of tea, the first thick in consistency, the second thin. Various interchanges also take place, in which guests admire the utensils and fittings chosen for the occasion. Choosing these appropriately can take a few days beforehand.

The *chashitsu*, as already explained, is smaller and more humble in character than an ordinary room. The main components are as follows: a floor of *tatami* mats, in different arrangements according to the size and the traditional formality of the setting; a sunken hearth (*ro*) set into the floor for heating the kettle in the winter season (in the summer, this is closed and a brazier used instead); an alcove (*tokonoma*) on the south side with a corner post (*tokobashira*) forming part of its frame; a scroll hanging on the *tokonoma* wall and either a flower or art object; a low small entrance (*nijiriguchi*) for guests to enter by crawling in; a separate entrance for the host with access to the preparation room or *mizuya*; one or more windows (*mado*) faced with a *shouji* screen of Japanese paper.

Visiting Japan now, the tea ceremony appears to have little relevance to most people's lives, particularly in cities like Tokyo and Osaka. Nevertheless, it embodies much of what the Japanese consider to be their cultural make-up, and the *chashitsu* is in some ways a glossary of architectural tradition. It is a reference for proportions, materials, and techniques. Since the collapse of the bubble economy in 1989 and the turning away from earlier design excesses, an increasing number of young architects and designers have been looking for inspiration to older traditions and crafts, and searching for ways to make them both modern and relevant. This goes some way towards explaining the revival of interest in the *chashitsu*. But there is more.

The Zen qualities of the tea-ceremony room imbue it with emptiness, both physically and conceptually. It therefore has elements of a blank space, a canvas for experiment. It has no requirements for the normal actions of living, which sets it apart from any other kind of dwelling space anywhere. It is, indeed, a special case in architecture, for I can think of no other category of space in any other culture which is on the one hand formally defined and yet non-functional in normal terms. Perhaps non-utilitarian would be a more accurate definition. One of the first Japanese architects to experiment boldly with the *chashitsu* was Arata Isozaki. He writes, "In 1983 the Leo Castelli Gallery in New York planned an exhibit of follies and asked architects to design structures like sculpture — aesthetic objects of no particular function as incidental compositional elements in a garden. When I received the invitation, I was thinking of the significance of arbors in East Asian gardens and of the tea house which is a space for a 'non-functional' tea ceremony, therefore similar to a folly." A decade later, Isozaki's drawings were turned into reality — the *chashitsu* called Ujian shown here on pages 128–135.

A traditional *sukiya*-style tea house re-assembled in the grounds of a new property designed by architect Kengo Kuma. The stones lead to the guests' entrance, known as the *nijiriguchi*, or crawling-in entrance. Next to the *nijiriguchi* is a bench where guests wait — the *machiai*. The larger host's entrance is to the left. At both entrances there are *kutsunugi-ishi* — a stone where shoes are removed.

A *tsukubai*, or stone water-basin, located on the path to the tea house on the previous pages. Its function is the ritual cleansing and purification of hands and mouth before entering the tea house.

The *chashitsu* also provides an opportunity to explore some of the more fundamental principles of architecture, without utilitarian restraints. For designer Shigeru Uchida, "The theme of Japanese space is 'change' ... The host creates a 'time' that is appropriate for the occasion in the empty space of a tea-room. He considers the taste of his guest and puts together a delicate balance of flowers, tools and meal to create an aesthetic beauty for that singular moment. Change is, in truth, newness, and the idea that eternity exists in the succession of newnesses was based on the 'sensory vibration' that disliked structuralization of architectures, and pursued delicate details." This thinking encouraged Uchida to explore simplicity, which he sees as a force in modern Japanese design for revealing the true nature of objects, and also what he considers "a subtle difference between the sense of space that a Japanese pursues and that western societies pursue." This led him to create a series of portable tea-ceremony rooms — light, ephemeral structures that can be sited in different locations so that the senses can take in the surroundings; as he puts it, "the natural vibrations such as the wind, sound, light and so on."

Another designer, Toshihiko Suzuki, echoes this appreciation of portability with the most moveable of all tea-ceremony rooms, one that folds into an aluminium carrying case (pages 236–237). "The original *chashitsu* were indeed portable", he explains. "They could be disassembled and moved. They were the earliest example of architecture as furniture, which is the area of ambiguity I'm exploring here." I raised the question of whether such radical re-interpretations of a long-established Japanese icon could be so extreme that they might find themselves completely outside the Way of Tea, something that Isozaki touched on when he said that he "thus risked creating disharmony". Suzuki replied, "When Murata Shuko and Sen no Rikyu challenged the elaborate and luxurious tea gatherings by making primitive, rustic huts and using ordinary everyday utensils, they were being revolutionary. Being radical is a part of the tradition."

Individual expression is also a part of the tradition. Sen no Rikyo, to whom all discussions of the tea ceremony and its spaces return, is regarded as having had a supreme aesthetic sense. In the seminal work *The Book of Tea*, written in 1906 by the Japanese scholar Kakuzo Okakura, is the story of a famous tea master of the early seventeenth century, Enshu Kobori, who "was complimented by his disciples on the admirable taste he had displayed in the choice of his collection. Said they, 'Each piece is such that no one could help admiring. It shows that you had better taste than had Rikyu, for his collection could only be appreciated by one beholder in a thousand.' Sorrowfully Enshu replied: 'This only proves how commonplace I am. The great Rikyu dared to love only those objects which personally appealed to him, whereas I unconsciously cater to the taste of the majority'."

This ultimately is the great architectural challenge taken up in these new *chashitsu* — to have sufficient knowledge and confidence to create an arrangement of space and materials that fulfils all the requirements of the tea ceremony, yet is individual. Isozaki likened the process to the planning of the tea ceremony itself, "an aesthetic of composition and arrangement.... It comprises materials not used in conventional buildings and the spaces must be made to proclaim themselves to create its own microcosm."

Finally, a word about terminology. The space, a room, has been in English variously called tea room, tea-ceremony room or tea house, and none of these sounds completely right, largely because tea in the

An aluminium suitcase unfolds to reveal a portable tea space designed by Toshihiko Suzuki, the precursor to the *chashitsu* shown on pages 236–237.

West has more mundane associations. While it is true that a formal English tea is ceremonial after a fashion, this is more to do with social behaviour than with any more deep-seated concept or belief. We have ways of holding tea-cups, rituals of pouring and steeping, and concerns over whether the milk is added first or later, but in comparison to the original purpose of *chanoyu* fairly superficial. "Tea room" sounds more like a genteel cafe of the mid-twentieth century, "tea-ceremony room" more like a staged performance, and "tea house" more like a garden ornament.

Nevertheless, while it might be more accurate to stick to Japanese terminology, it would also get in the way of easy reading. So, for the *chashitsu* itself I use two English terms. When it is free-standing, as used to be normal but now, in space-deprived Japan, very rare, I call it a tea house; when part of a house or apartment, which is the case with the majority of these new designs, I use the term tea-ceremony room. There is also an important distinction between a room that is designed solely for the tea ceremony — *chashitsu* — and one that is also used less strictly, and I'm indebted to architect Chitoshi Kihara for explaining this. It was considered one of Sen no Rikyu's great achievements that towards the end of his life he was able to reduce the *chashitsu* to such essentials that it could only be used for this exact purpose. Modern life in Japan places such pressure on space that even devoting one room to the traditional *tatami* style is a luxury. As a result, a number of the spaces here are dual, or even multi-purpose, and these are more properly called *washitsu*, for which I also use the expression *tatami* room.

The tea-ceremony room

Plan of middle-size tea-ceremony room with four
and a half *tatami* mats (*yojouhan*)

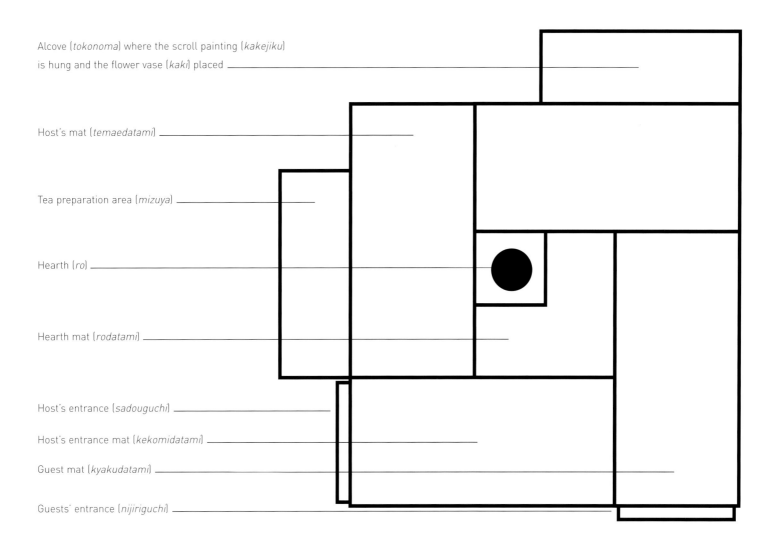

Alcove (*tokonoma*) where the scroll painting (*kakejiku*)
is hung and the flower vase (*kaki*) placed

Host's mat (*temaedatami*)

Tea preparation area (*mizuya*)

Hearth (*ro*)

Hearth mat (*rodatami*)

Host's entrance (*sadouguchi*)

Host's entrance mat (*kekomidatami*)

Guest mat (*kyakudatami*)

Guests' entrance (*nijiriguchi*)

Glossary

Cha: tea; tea ceremony; the study of tea

Chabana: simple style of flower arranging used in tea ceremony

Chado (also *sado*): the ritual art of preparing green tea; the Way of Tea

Chaire: container for *koicha* powdered tea

Chaji: full tea ceremony with a *kaiseki* meal, lasting three–five hours

Chakai: short tea ceremony that does not involve *kaiseki* meal, lasting twenty minutes–one hour

Chakin: rectangular, white linen or hemp cloth used to ritually cleanse the tea bowl

Chaniwa: tea garden

Chanoyu: see *chado*

Chasen: whisk carved from bamboo used to blend powdered tea and water

Chashaku: tea scoop carved from bamboo

Chashitsu: tea-ceremony room

Chawan: bowl for drinking tea

Chigaidana: staggered shelves

Chumon: small middle gate dividing outer and inner tea gardens, symbolising door between physical world and spiritual world of tea

—

Daime: *tatami* mat about three-quarters the length of standard mat; usually used for the host's mat

Dougu: equipment for tea ceremony

—

Fukusa: square, silk cloth used for ritual cleaning of tea equipment and handling hot lids

Furo: portable hearth for use during the summer months in place of the *ro*, or sunken hearth

Futaoki: green bamboo rest for the kettle lid

—

Goza: second part of a *chaji* full tea ceremony

—

Hanto: assistant to the tea master

Higashi: dry sweets served during the ceremony with thin tea

Hishaku: long bamboo tea ladle

Hiroma: large tea-ceremony room over four and half *tatami* mats

—

Iemoto: head of tea school; founder of tea school

—

Kama: iron pot used for heating water

Kaiseki ryori: type of food served during tea ceremony

Kakejiku (also *kakemono*): scroll painting hanging in the *tokonoma*

Kaki: flower vase placed or hanging inside the *tokonoma*

Kekomidatami: host's entrance mat

Kensui: waste water bowl

Kinindatami: nobleman's mat

Koicha: thick tea

Koma: small tea-ceremony room containing two to four and half *tatami* mats

Koshikake machiai: bench for guests to wait before being called to the *chashitsu*

Kougou: incense container

Kutsunugi-ishi: stone where shoes are removed at the entrance to the room

Kyakudatami: guest mat

—

Machiai: waiting area outside the *chashitsu* for guests to sit

Mado: window

Matcha: powdered green tea

Mizusashi: water jug

Mizuya: preparation area; room where host gathers and prepares equipment

Mushanokojisenke: one of three main schools of tea ceremony

—

Natsume: date-shaped wooden container for *usucha* powdered tea

Nakabashira: central pillar in a tea-ceremony room

Nijiriguchi: small, low entrance through which guests crawl into the tea room, thereby inducing humility

Nijou: two normal size *tatami* mats

Nijoudaime: two normal size *tatami* mats plus one smaller (*daime*)

Nodate: open-air improvised version of the tea ceremony

Omotesenke: one of three main schools of tea ceremony

—

Ranma: transom

Ro: hearth set into the floor used in winter

Rodatami: hearth mat

Roji: literally "dewy ground"; garden path to the tea house

Ryureiseki: a less formal tea ceremony with tables and chairs

—

Sabi: Aesthetic term meaning beauty or serenity that comes with age

Sadouguchi (also *chatateguchi*): host's entrance

Sanjou: three normal size *tatami* mats

Sanjoudaime: three normal size *tatami* mats plus one smaller (*daime*)

Sayu: hot water used in making tea

Sencha-do: informal tea style in which boiled water is poured over tea leaves

Shouji: room divider made of translucent *washi* paper over a wooden frame

Souan: small thatched hut used for tea ceremonies in fifteenth century

Shoza: first part of a *chaji* full tea ceremony, during which a light meal is served

Sumi: charcoal

—

Tatami: traditional floor unit made of *igusa* rushes

Teishu: tea-ceremony master

Temae-za: space for making tea

Temaedatami (also *dougudatami*): *tatami* mat for the host

Tetsubin: iron teapot-shaped pot for heating water

Tokonoma: alcove in tea room where scrolls are hung

Tokobashira: corner pillar by the side of the *tokonoma*

Tsukeshoin: built-in table

Tsukubai: stone water-basin for washing and purifying hands and mouth

—

Urasenke: one of the three main schools of tea ceremony

Usucha: thin tea

—

Wabi: aesthetic term meaning quiet or sober refinement, or subdued taste

Wabi-sabi: a beauty that is imperfect, impermanent, and incomplete

Wabisuki: aesthetic term for simple taste

Wagashi: confectionery

Washitsu: traditional *tatami* room, which can be converted for use as a *chashitsu*

—

Yojou: four normal *tatami* mats

Yojouhan: middle size tea-ceremony room of four and a half *tatami* mats

—

Zabuton: cushions for guests

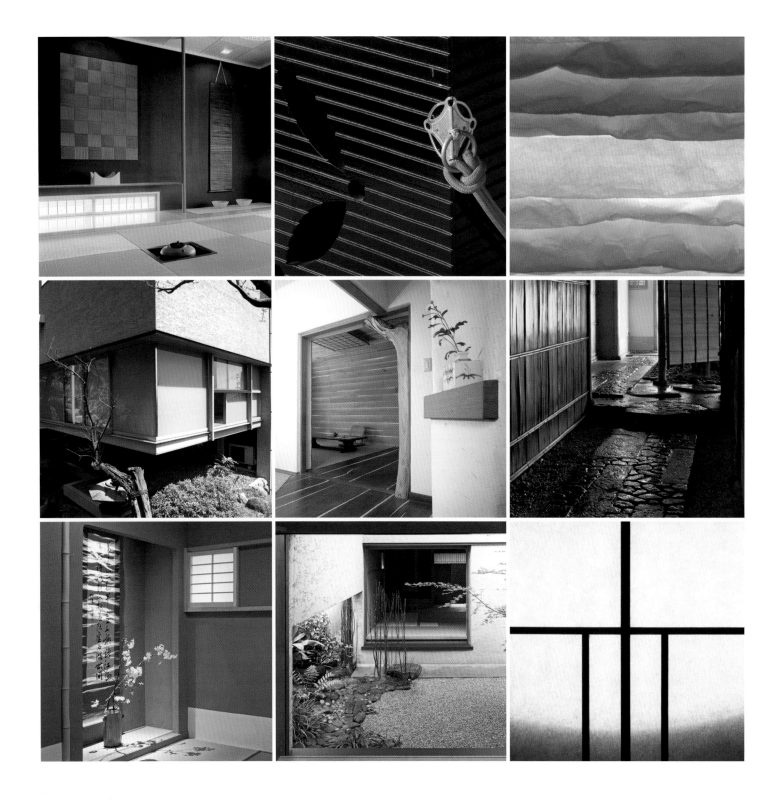

New
Traditional

Choshoan

location: Hotel Okura, Minato-ku, Tokyo

architects: Sotoji Nakamura + Yoshiro Taniguchi

date: 2004

The short approach path to the tea room is unusually from inside the hotel – a kind of interior *roji*.

Right:
In this more modern style of tea ceremony, the occasion is conducted seated – Western style. This table is for the tea master.

Built into the Okura Hotel in Tokyo in 1963, this was one of the first "modern" tea-ceremony rooms, designed as part of a new hotel and featuring notable design changes to its inspiration — an old tea house called Yuin (hut) linked to Urasenke, the largest tea-ceremony school. The original, built in the mid-seventeenth century by Sen Sotan, the grandson of Sen no Rikyu, is considered to be the basis of the *souan yojouhan* — a small, rustic style tea-ceremony structure of up to four and a half *tatami* mats, used to perform a simple, quiet ceremony. The hotel, built in time for the 1964 Tokyo Olympics, was the first in Japan to incorporate a tea-ceremony room, and has recently been renovated. The detailing was by master carpenter and expert artisan Sotoji Nakamura (see also Ujian on pages 128–135) and the project was overseen and managed by Yoshiro Taniguchi. One important difference is that while plain boards covered with a wickerwork mat (*ajiro tenjou*) were used for the ceiling of Yuin, here there is a coffered ceiling with ribs framing recessed panels (*goutenjou*), using a variety of reed, bamboo grass, and straw, in a rich, harmonious arrangement. The flooring is of a high quality cedar from Kitayama known as *Kitayama no migaki maruta*. The room is set out for *ryureiseki*, the form of tea ceremony where guests can sit on chairs (popular with those who cannot sit in *seiza* — the traditional kneeling position). The room is named Chosho after the pen name of the hotel's owner, Kishichiro Okura. In the same tea house there is also a more traditionally designed *chashitsu* available for guests.

The seating arrangement for three guests, with a long, low table in front of the *zabuton* cushions. The calligraphy is by Jian-ou Matsunaga, a highly influential figure in the tea ceremony world.

The *chawan*, or bowl for whisking the *matcha*, or powdered green tea, with a traditionally made bamboo whisk.

A second *chashitsu*, more traditionally designed, with the alcove on the right and a calligraphy scroll.

Detail of the wooden diffusing grid on one of the floor lamps.

A *hishaku*, or ladle carved from a bamboo culm, with a slice of bamboo for a handle, resting on the black lacquer surface of the table.

Detail of the carved black lacquer of the tea master's table.

Aura Chaya

location: Ikoma, Nara
architect: Michinobu Nonomura
date: 2006

This tea-ceremony room was designed as a fusion of traditional form and new materials, specifically materials made by the client, Aura Limited. These include *odoshishikoro*, a newly invented leather material made of very thin leather strips treated with fluorine as a water- and stain-repellent, woven together into a fabric, and here used on the rear wall as a hanging to replace the traditional *kakejiku*, or scroll painting that hangs in the *tokonoma* recess. The term comes from two kinds of traditional armour — *odoshi*, small plates woven together, and *shikoro*, a neck guard. The prominent red of the pillar is from a traditional dyed braiding technique known as *kumihimo*, but here applied to rayon instead of the usual silk; the cord is wound tightly around a vertical pole. On the left wall is another hanging work — a chequerboard arrangement of smoked tiles, with a characteristic lustre that occurs when films of carbon are deposited on their surface in the smoking process. The blown glass bowls are reproductions of works by designer Eisuke Kashiwazaki.

Red braiding replaces the traditional rough wood of the alcove's corner post, or *tokobashira*.

The spacious *chashitsu* functions as a subtle display space for new materials produced by the sponsoring company, Aura.

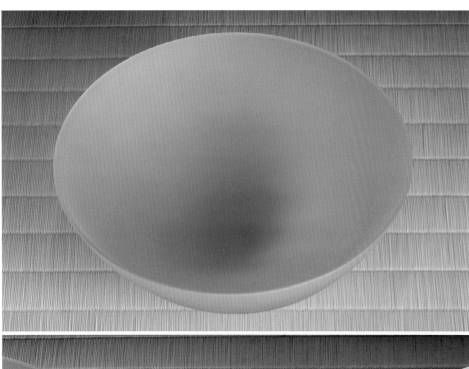

Frosted glass bowls on *tatami* matting are reproductions of those by Eisuke Kashiwazaki (1910–1986), a leading designer who worked to develop the craft industries of Fukuoka.

The *mizuya*, or service area, with water supply and utensils.

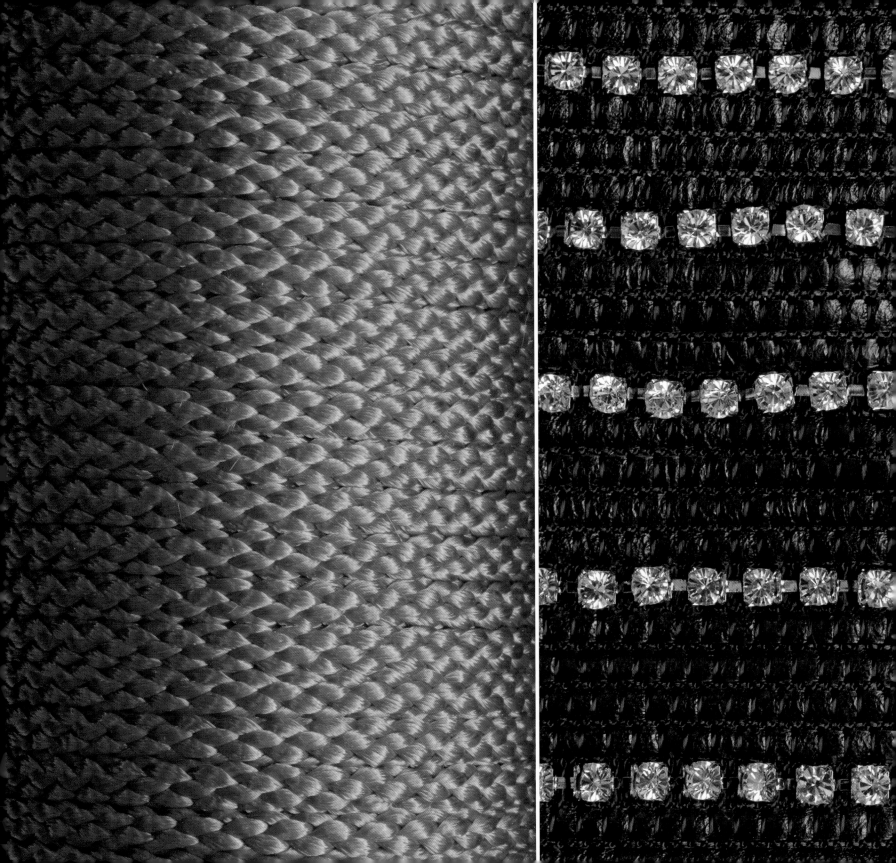

A medley of new materials developed by the company Aura based on traditional methods. From left to right: red rayon cord, woven leather with sewn-in crystals, and a gossamer-like hand-made paper.

Seifuan (Clear Wind)

location: Sendagaya, Tokyo
architect: Atsushi Kitagawara
date: 1997

Architect Atsushi Kitagawara built this tea-ceremony room for his own use, in a modern, free-form version of the *sukiya*-style, marked by rustic simplicity and use of natural materials. The mud-plaster *arakabe* walls are somewhat darker than usual, rendered with mud collected from rice fields in Shinshu, mixed together with straw from local farmers. The *tatami* mats are from the Ryukyu Islands in the far southwest and are without the normal edging — they were selected to give a neater and larger impression to the space. The ceiling is covered with hand-laid *washi* paper that has been rolled and gummed into tubes around long sticks cut from bamboo (Kitagawara's architectural students were given this job), and this light structure softens the ceiling lights. Natural light is also diffused by *washi* paper — a large sheet, crumpled and curved in front of the window. There is neither *tokonoma* nor hanging scroll painting, as Kitagawara and his wife prefer a relaxed and informal style of tea ceremony. Instead, he chooses whatever display he thinks is appropriate for his guests, and in the setting shown here, a framed print by a photographer friend Yuriko Takagi was placed against the wall. Flowers are always taken from the terrace garden, and here are *Tricyris hirta* (Japanese Toad Lily) and a twig of blueberry.

The sunken square hearth in the floor is for the iron kettle. The long photograph against the wall takes the place of a traditional display in an alcove.

The simplicity of natural materials is characteristic of the *sukiya*-style of tea-ceremony room, here in contemporary form.

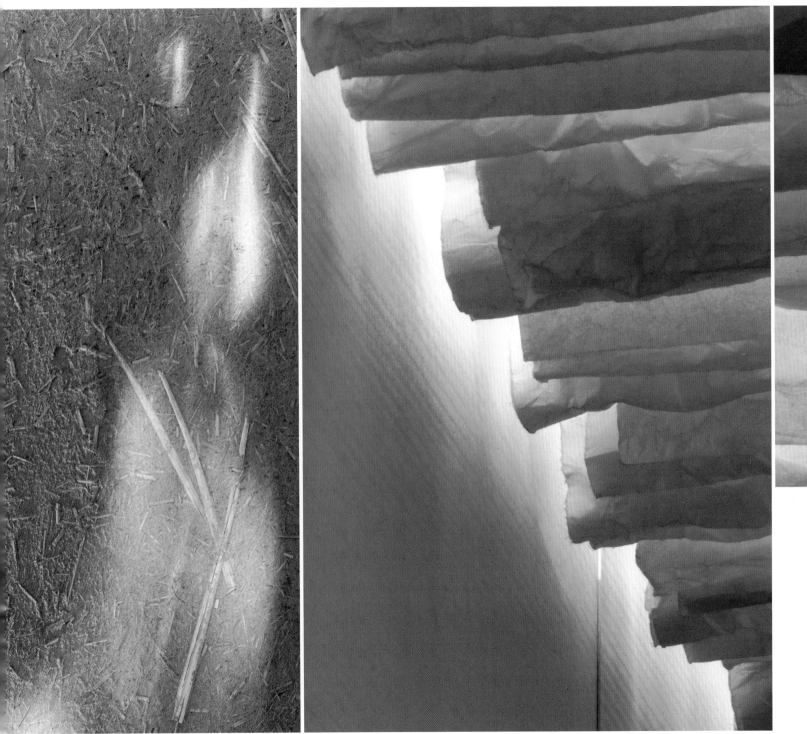

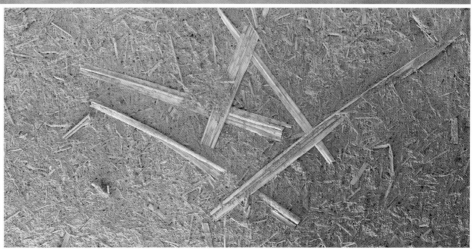

Natural earthen colours create an atmosphere of warmth and simplicity. The walls are plastered with a mixture of clay, sand and straw known as *arakabe-tsuchi*. Handmade *washi* paper makes an unusual appearance in the form of rolled tubes that conceal and modulate the ceiling lights.

Sannocho-no-ie

location: Sannocho, Hyogo

architect/designer: Chitoshi Kihara

+ Yasujirou Aoki

date: 2002

This large (*hachijou* or eight-*tatami* mat) combined *washitsu* and *chashitsu* is suspended over an old hillside garden in Kansai, the western part of Japan. The original house was badly damaged in the Great Hanshin earthquake of 1995, and for the new construction the client wanted to make the most of the view with a design that was modern, but yet respected Japanese traditions. After discussions, it was agreed to keep the old rock garden with its pond rather than cut into the cliff, and Kihara proposed siting the *washitsu* in the most favourable position for a view of the trees and cliff, on the lower level but cantilevered out over the water. Referring to Frank Lloyd Wright's design for Fallingwater house in America, which is built over rather than opposite a waterfall, Kihara says, "Similarly, I chose to create a Japanese

The cantilevering allows the room to project into the surrounding landscape. The architect designed a floor-to-ceiling arrangement of frosted glass and *shouji* screens that open in various permutations to take full advantage of this.

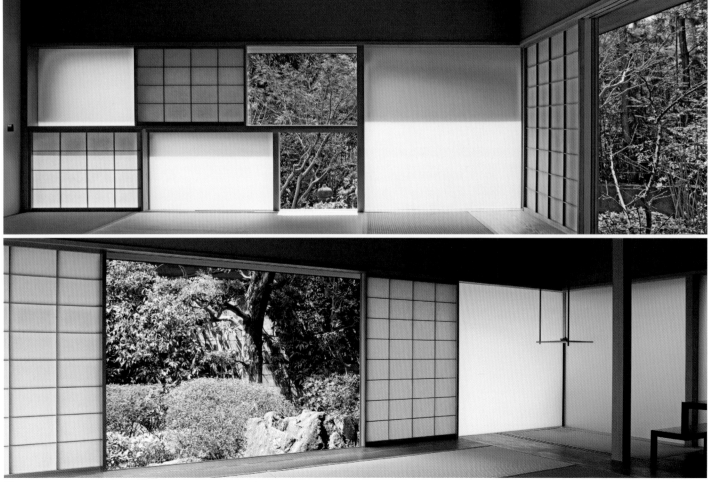

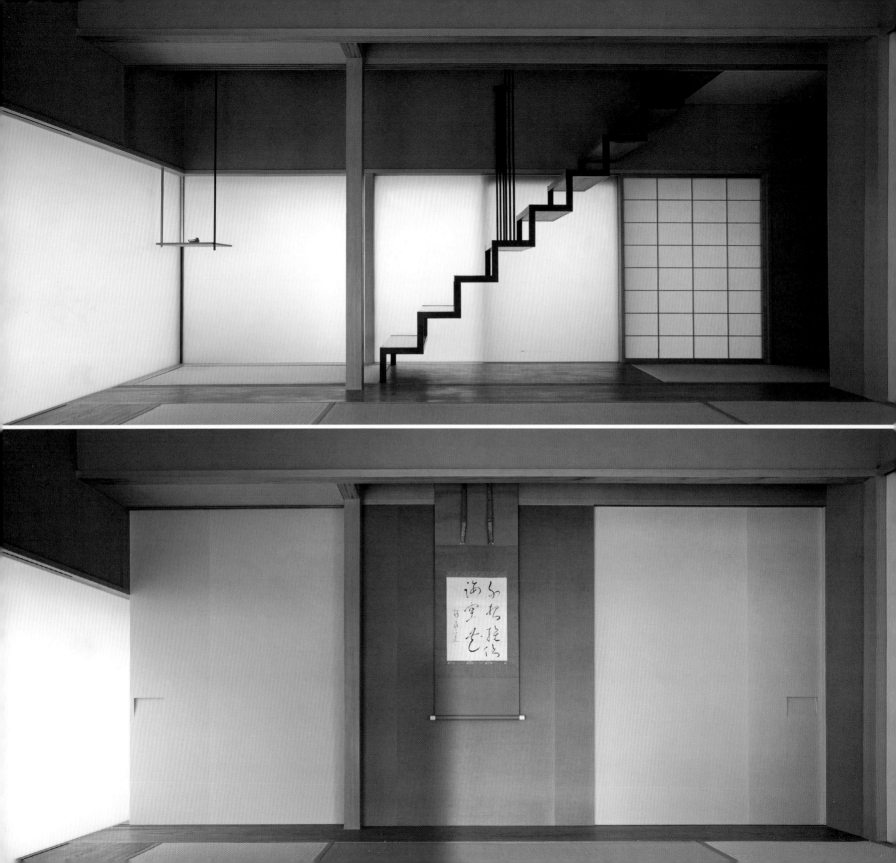

room above the pond rather than with a view of it." A minimal, suspended steel staircase with wooden steps descends to it from the main living and dining area of the house on the floor above. The *washitsu* is adaptable in that the screens on the two sides that project over the garden can be opened fully to connect with the natural surroundings, or closed for a more formal atmosphere. The space is also adaptable — panels recessed into the wall can slide out to close off the staircase and frosted glass windows behind, and allow it function as a tea-ceremony room.

Far left:
Sliding panels which recess into the wall at right reconfigure the room from a light and airy modern *tatami* room into a more formal *chashitsu*. Concealed fixtures are in place for hanging the *kakejiku* or scroll.

Access to the *washitsu* is from the floor above. The open staircase of steel with wooden steps and no risers contributes a floating feeling to the room.

The play of light changes with the time and weather. As the sun rises, its reflections from the pond in the garden below flicker over the frosted glass panel. The calligraphy on the scroll is by Ryokan, a Zen Priest, poet, and calligrapher of Soudou-shu from the Edo era.

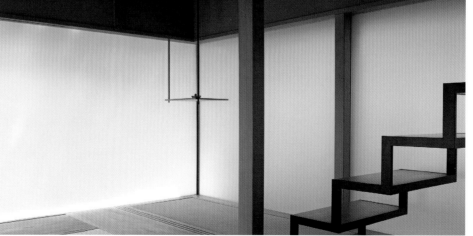

A minimal steel and glass display shelf hangs in the corner, carrying a small *kougou* or incense container (left). The view from the top of the staircase with its curved brass rail (above).

Yokoo-tei

location: Chichibu, Saitama

designer: Takao Fujiki

date: 2004

This is a simple and personal *chashitsu* built into the combined studio and residence of the painter and sculptor Tatsuhiko Yokoo, constructed on the edge of the mountainous Chichibu-Tama-Kai National Park. The room adjoins the double-height studio space, and Yokoo regularly practises Zen meditation here. The *tokonoma* is the principal point of difference in this minimal space, with an unfinished but polished rear wall of concrete that still retains the formwork fittings, and in place of the normal *kakejiku*, or hanging scroll, a small work by the artist. The alcove post is of Japanese cedar roughly planed, and the plaster walls are in *juraku* style. There are many different kinds of earthen plaster wall in Japanese building according to the mixture, origin, and application. The brown plaster here, originally from Nishijin, Kyoto, is a simplified version of *juraku-kabe* (*juraku* wall), and is highly regarded for *chashitsu*.

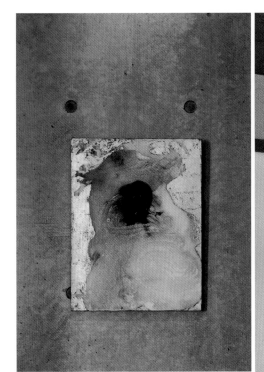

On the first floor of the building, the room serves as a connector between residence and atelier, and also, in its mix of concrete, *tatami*, plaster, and *shina* veneer, between modern and classical Japanese style. The small painting with gold leaf in the alcove is by the artist.

Fujiidera-no-ie

location: Fujiidera, Osaka

architect/designer: Chitoshi Kihara
+ Yasujirou Aoki

date: 2000

While a scroll hangs in the normal position for a *tokonoma*, or display recess, the curved red-enamelled steel wall dominates the view. A flower vase, or *kaki*, hangs in its centre.

The sliding *shouji* screens can be set to create different visual effects. Slightly opened, they reveal the enamelled wall as a strip, reflected in the low black lacquer table.

Above and left:
Two modern variations on the
theme of the slat patterns found
on paper screens, or *shouji*.

Osaka-based architect Chitoshi Kihara, who also designed the rooms Sannocho-no-ie and Mihara-no-ie (pages 44–49, 160–163), here created a *chashitsu* with a focal point completely in contrast to the normal principles of restraint and natural colours, but with a specific purpose. The most striking visual feature, and central to its theme, is the scarlet curved stainless steel wall which is just outside the room and dominates it when the *shouji* screens are pulled back even slightly. Here this takes the place of the *tokonoma*. In Japan this particular red, known as *hiiro*, is a celebratory colour with associations of good fortune, and Kihara chose it at the client's request to create an atmosphere of positive brightness to help when his wife was diagnosed with cancer. Precisely, it is the red of *himosen* (literally, the colour of a sundew plant), which is the cloth used at festivals and weddings, and also to spread on the ground for *nodate*, the open-air improvised version of the tea ceremony. Another, plum-coloured, red was chosen for the hanging scroll instead of the more usual calligraphy. The *tatami* mats are of the special three-quarter size made for tea-ceremony rooms known as *daime*, and seven cover the area here.

A granite *tsukubai*, or water basin, for washing hands before entering the tea-ceremony room.

The small low entrance to the room seen from the other side of a central garden courtyard.

57

Tampopo House (Dandelions)

location: Tokyo

architect: Terunobu Fujimori

date: 1997

For his own house in Tokyo, architect and professor at Tokyo University Terunobu Fujimori, who also designed the unusual tea-ceremony rooms on pages 200–203 and 230–235, created a room which echoes some of the rusticity of the traditional *sukiya* style, but idiosyncratically. This is a *washitsu* that can, when needed, be used for the tea ceremony, although it is filled with light from two windows. Notably, he used rough wooden planking for all the walls and ceiling, as well as for the floor in the corridor outside, filling in the spaces between them with white plaster. The floor covering for the *washitsu* is split-bamboo matting. Fujimori practices a unique form of architecture, using natural materials and aiming for a "comprehensive" vernacular style. His principal concern, and the subject of most of his writings, is the need to incorporate nature into modern buildings. This, his own house, is named after the dandelions (*tampopo*) that are carefully nurtured in rows covering the exterior. "My dream", he has said, "is to grow plants on buildings just as the human body grows hair."

The façade of the Tampopo House, covered in dandelions and grass.

The *washitsu*, lined with rough planking, with an iron kettle (*kama*) in the sunken *ro*, or hearth.

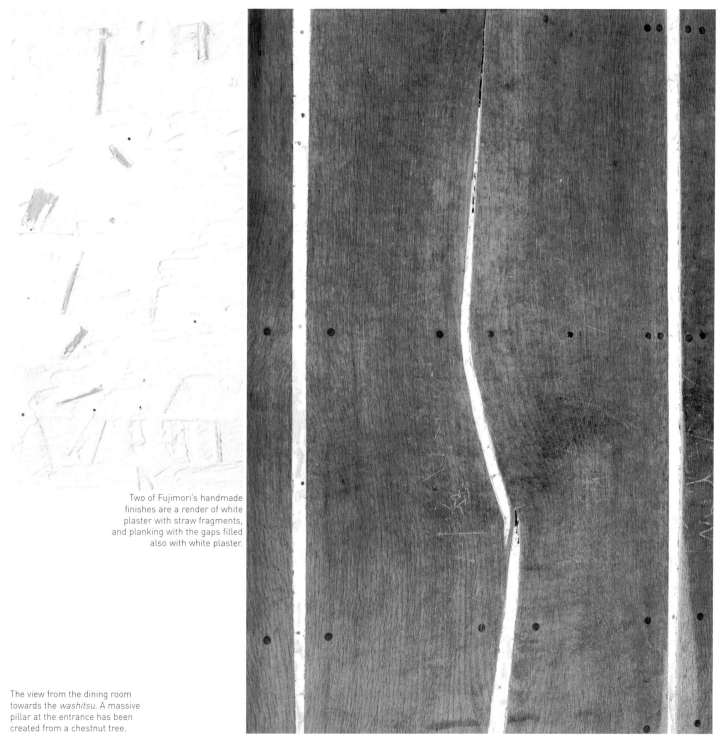

Two of Fujimori's handmade finishes are a render of white plaster with straw fragments, and planking with the gaps filled also with white plaster.

The view from the dining room towards the *washitsu*. A massive pillar at the entrance has been created from a chestnut tree.

Zekuan

location: Kita-ku, Tokyo
architect: Michimasa Kawaguchi
date: 2005

Part of a house designed at the client's request in a modern Japanese style, this *chashitsu* maintains tradition in materials with subtly modernised proportions and detailing. A concealed staircase outside the entrance leads up to a small room designed as a study/retreat, hidden away from the rest of the house. Architect Kawaguchi, who also designed the tea-ceremony room on pages 68–71, has a great love of the traditional craft component of Japanese building, and researches closely the many techniques in rendering and carpentry. The plaster render is a variety of the traditional *shikkui* lime plaster known as *tosa-shikkui*, in which there is no glue or gum so that it is more water resistant, and which has a gentle and natural yellowish colour that is becoming increasingly rare in modern construction. Bamboo and red cedar are also used in the room.

As with many other *chashitsu*, this was given a unique name, and it is taken from the Buddhist expression "shiki soku ze ku", which translates approximately as "all is vanity", referring to the transience of life. This was poignantly suggested by the day on which the contract was signed with the architect — September 11, 2001. As the house is a fusion of Japanese and Western design, this name is written in a combination of Chinese characters and Roman — a small but significant point.

The offset arrangement of two small sliding windows covered in *shouji* contributes to the modern appearance of the *chashitsu*. The yellow *seto-yaki* pot in the alcove is by Hidetake Ando.

63

Sliding panels immediately
outside the *chashitsu* open for
access to a ladder leading up
to a hidden room above.

Following pages:
Pairs of bamboo lengths lashed together form the screen of a window to the corridor (close-up detail far right). A magnified view of the plaster wall in the corridor reveals fragments of straw.

A concealed small room directly above the tea room performs an additional lighting function, with a skylight above a translucent floor panel.

A sliding *shouji* screen with a modern design of wooden slats.

Sara

location: Asakusa, Tokyo

architect: Michimasa Kawaguchi

date: 2004

This *washitsu*, in a house designed by architect Michimasa Kawaguchi, features subtle revivals of old architectural traditions. Kawaguchi has a deserved reputation for re-interpreting traditions and materials. Here he developed the idea of a *toritsugi-no-ma*, which was a room for guests to wait in on arrival, similar to the early function of an English parlour. He designed a low window, protected by sliding shutters, to look out onto the stairwell. In summer the window allows a breeze to move through the room. The wall is rendered in a traditional finish, lightly coloured sand plaster known as *suna-shikkui*. Typically in Japan, especially in temples, this is covered with white plaster which, over time, wears away from exteriors to reveal the *suna-shikkui* underneath. This part-worn appearance evokes a certain nostalgia — for example, when the famous Kyoto temple Ryoan-ji had its walls restored to a fresh white in 1989, many felt that this was a loss. Kawaguchi here recreates this patina with the old sand render. Another feature with references to the past is the style of *shouji* screen, in which the vertical slats are spaced in close pairs. Kawaguchi intended this as a gentle reminder of the Edo era in the Asakusa area of Tokyo. This was the famous *shitamachi*, or downtown, and this style of *shouji* was considered quite smart and stylish at the time — and was often used to decorate brothels.

A small niche with downlighter is recessed into the wall and finished in the same sand plaster render.

On the first floor of the narrow, four-storey house, the small *washitsu* is the first residential room that visitors see, glimpsed through the low sliding oak shutters.

Shimakin

location: Kagurazaka, Tokyo
architect: Fujio Takayama
date: 2004

In the basement of a long-established traditional restaurant, called Shimakin, in the Kagurazaka district of central Tokyo, architect Fujio Takayama was commissioned to design three adjoining tea-ceremony rooms that could be used for tea ceremonies as well as for meetings and seminars. In three different sizes, each room has a specific character: the largest, called Shou fu ken, representing "village", has a floor area of *jujou* (ten *tatami* mats) with the *tatami* laid in parallel for a spacious feeling. The smallest, called San-an, meaning "mountain", is by contrast only *nijoudaime* (two normal and one three-quarter size *tatami*), and has a calm, quiet character. The third, Kaigetsu-tei, representing "ocean", is the most striking, with a wickerwork ceiling, loosely woven from white bamboo (*shiratake*). Particular care went into the lighting design (which received several awards), with diffused fluorescent strip-lighting over the woven bamboo ceiling in Kaigetsu-tei, and backlit acrylic panels pasted over with traditional Japanese paper in Shou fu ken.

The largest of the three rooms is called Shou fu ken, with a sloping ceiling, square-sectioned alcove pillar, and a calligraphy scroll from Eihei-ji temple with a poem about a novice monk's long journey.

72

Previous pages left:
The staircase down from street level. The wall is in pine finished by shaving with a hand-axe.

Previous pages right:
The most prominent feature of Kaigetsu-tei – which has a floor area of *hachijou* (eight mats) – is its ceiling of woven bamboo supported on a metal frame and lit from above. The calligraphy is about the metempsychosis of birds and flowers.

Left:
San-an is the smallest of the three *chashitsu*, viewed here from the crawling-in entrance. The scroll is by Shiba Ko, a calligrapher from the local Kagurazaka area.

Above:
A decorative arrangement of objects in Shou fu ken, in a second, backlit recess next to the *tokonoma*.

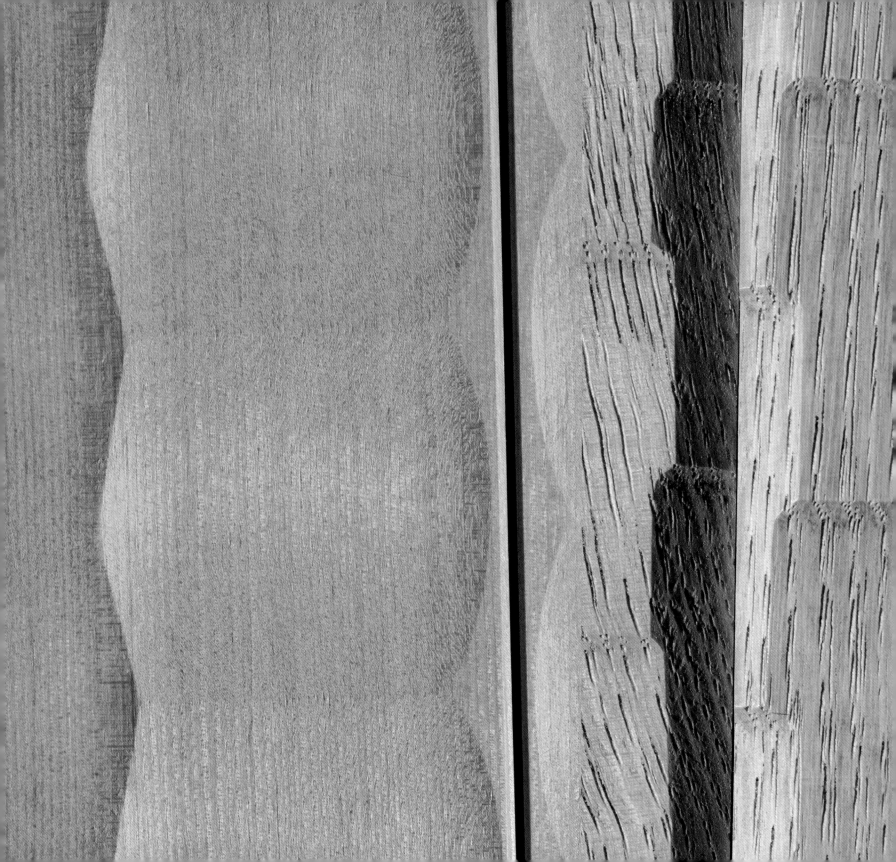

The simple ceramic flower container, or *kaki*, in Kaigetsu-tei has an equally simple spring arrangement of cherry and gymnaster. The small purple flowers of the latter were named *miyako wasure*, meaning "Forgetting [Kyoto]" by the deposed emperor Juntoku when in exile.

Left:
Details of the carved chestnut wall of the waiting area for the three *chashitsu*.

Modern
Materials

Kumon

location: Chayu Club Kumon, Nihonbashi, Tokyo
architect: Fujio Takayama
date: 1995

These two adjacent tea-ceremony rooms were installed in an institute for the promotion of the tea ceremony in a downtown office building in Tokyo. The objective of the institute is to offer people who might otherwise think the tea ceremony too rigorous or costly the opportunity to experience the ceremony informally. As part of this approach, it was decided to construct the *chashitsu* in a contemporary way so as to give an immediate impression to visitors of the relevance of the Way of Tea in modern life. Architect Fujio Takayama chose transparent acrylic for the principal material as a solution in his search for "a space that would facilitate communication between the tea master and guests with the minimum obstruction." In particular, he chose a transparent material to emphasise the aspect of "emptiness" that is important in the Zen interpretation of the tea-ceremony room. Acrylic was preferred to glass because the latter would introduce refracted colour at its edges (that is, be less transparent and "empty"), and also for safety reasons. Takayama feels that there is strong justification for constructing tea-ceremony rooms "casually, using materials common in the current era." The precision of construction was actually more demanding than if wood had been used throughout, as in the latter case on-site adjustments, by planing and sanding, would have been easier to make. However, an advantage of acrylic resin is that restoration of the surfaces is straightforward — scratches can be polished out.

Clear acrylic pillars are combined with walls of thin steel with Japanese paper to give the construction lightness. This first *chashitsu* is *sanjou*, meaning three *tatami* mats in size.

Right:
Acrylic panels covered with Japanese paper form the ceiling, diffusing light from above.

Following pages:
Contiguous with the first room, but separated by sliding panels is this *hachijou* (eight *tatami*-mat) room. A suspended acrylic unit with shelf and green-tinted vertical panels supports utensils.

Quan (Empty)

location: portable

architect/designer: Hisanobu Tsujimura + Soushin Kimura

date: 2006

This glass-walled *chashitsu*, portable like that of Shigeru Uchida on pages 192–199, was the creation of Osaka-based designer Hisanobu Tsujimura, and first exhibited in Milan in 2005. The "Qu", with its unusual Roman spelling chosen by the designer, means "vacant", "empty", "blank" and Tsujimura expresses his concept as follows:

Being never exceeds nothingness.
Emptiness is relative, but it generates perfect harmony.
It is not an instrument to be used, but a state to be experienced.
It is not a design, but the foundation of an affinity.

The construction materials are glass, bamboo, and handmade paper, with a special tatami flooring designed by Tsujimura. The edging to the mats, instead of the traditional cloth, is an LED (light-emitting diodes) strip, which glows brightly and evenly when seen from above. Moulded acrylic stepping stones are also lit from within by LEDs. The construction, and formal aspects of the design, were supervised for Tsujimura by professional tea master Soushin Kimura.

The *tatami* mat edging, here seen surrounding the hearth, utilises 0.3 mm-thick flexible LED strips.

Far right:
The *chashitsu*, in light materials, seen here at a design show in Tokyo, can be easily dismantled and re-erected.

Looking down from the *chashitsu* to the glowing moulded stepping stones.

Heisei-no-nijoudaime

location: Kawagoe, Saitama
architect: Ken Yokogawa
date: 2004

This tea room is in one of the oldest temples in the historic town of Kawagoe, founded in the thirteenth century. The temple decided to have built a tea room that was unique and in a modern idiom — representing the current Heisei era (which began with Emperor Akihito's reign in 1989) — and so held a competition for the design. The winning entry, by architect Ken Yokogawa, includes the *roji*, or garden approach, and waiting area for guests. This is in the form of an open structure built around existing zelkova and ginkgo trees with shallow pebble-filled ponds; circular holes cut into the roof accommodate the trees. A curved bench of Brazilian hardwood sited halfway along this open sheltered area functions as the *machiai*, for guests to wait and contemplate before being called to the tea-ceremony room. This small house, with a notably tiny *nijiriguchi*, or "crawling-in entrance", is in concrete, aluminium, and glass. The etched glass walls, one of them creating what is essentially a backlit *tokonoma*, have laid over them specially designed handmade Japanese rice paper — *tesuki-washi* from Echizen. Concealed lighting below an opalescent ledge adds to the translucency, while the end wall can be opened to provide visual connection with the trees and ponds.

The final section of the *roji*, with the *chashitsu* at far left, seen from the side.

Following pages left:
At the end of the *roji*, close by one of the old zelkova trees, stepping stones cross the shallow pond to the low entrance to the *chashitsu*.

Following pages right:
The view back from the *chashitsu*. The temple grounds continue to the right.

The *tsukubai* has been cut
vertically in half, then
re-assembled sandwiching a
thick sheet of glass.

The final stepping stone is made of 60-mm sheets of baked, frosted glass that have been layered and then finally chiselled.

Following pages:
Combining acrylic and different patterns of handmade paper, Yokogawa created an interior fusion of new and old.

Previous pages:
The front wall is made of
5 mm-thick aluminium, with
panels that hinge open; the
side wall is of strengthened
glass to which hand-made
paper has been attached.

Left:
The room seen from the
"crawling-in entrance". The
central pillar is composed of
ebony, Bombay blackwood,
maple, and aluminium, sanded
and routed together.

Above:
The base of the *tokonoma* is in
opalescent plastic, lit from below.

99

Cha Ginza

location: Ginza, Tokyo

architect: Shigeru Uchida

date: 2005

Sunlight throws shadows of the ceiling's steel girders on one wall. The *chashitsu* is open to the sky and the elements.

Shigeru Uchida is possibly Japan's best-known designer — of products, furniture, and spaces. His major works include the Wave Building in Roppongi and a series of Yohji Yamamoto's boutiques. Since the end of the 1990s, Uchida has designed several quite radical tea-ceremony rooms, a subject that fascinates him because of its fundamental importance to Japanese architecture and the Japanese perception of space. As he explains, "The theme of Japanese space is 'change'. The interior was used in various ways depending on the time or occasion of day, and was transformed accordingly." Applying this principle to the top floor of an upmarket tea shop and tea rooms in fashionable Ginza, Uchida created a *chashitsu* in an urban setting, with a roof spanned by steel girders and open to the sky. The client wanted a *chashitsu* laid out for the less formal *ryureiseki*, with table and seating, yet also metropolitan in flavour and using contemporary materials and designers' products. Brushed aluminium walls and a stained wooden floor provide the setting. The egg-shaped lamp, in opal polyethylene resin and appropriately titled "l'uovo", was designed by Uchida for manufacturer Yamagiwa.

Mizusashi (water jug) by ceramic artist Katsue Ibata.

The host's table, with kettle in its hearth, water container and other utensils.

The *chashaku* (bamboo ladle for drawing water from the kettle and water jar) is by Makoto Ito, and rests on a ceramic *futaoki* (a rest for the ladle and kettle lid).

Detail of the contemporary *kaki*, or flower container, by glass artist Setsuko Miura.

The tea-room at night: the name of the *chashitsu* – Kuukai – is in calligraphy by Uchida on the spotlit scroll painting, and illuminated by the designer's "egg" floor lamp.

Shunju

location: Roppongi, Tokyo
designer: Takashi Sugimoto
year: 2001

Located, perhaps surprisingly, in a restaurant in the heart of Roppongi, this small *chashitsu* in steel is the creation of one of Japan's leading interior designers, Takashi Sugimoto, who founded his now well-known design company Super Potato in 1973. Specialising in restaurants, hotels, and shops, Sugimoto understands the value of lighting and rich combinations of materials in creating atmosphere and a strong spatial sense. Like his design for the *chashitsu* in the Niki Club resort on pages 120–127, this two-*tatami chashitsu* (*nijouhan*) incorporates steel openwork — layers of burnished grilles — but here he also combines it with etched solid panels in a variety of textures. Material texture is, in fact, the dominant theme, and the industrial finish of the steel contrasts strikingly with a section of traditional earthen wall and the *tatami* mats.

Interior of Shunju Restaurant in the middle of Roppongi, Tokyo.

Below left:
One wall is made of steel sheets that have been pitted by acid.

Below right:
Another wall has a lattice effect created using burnished steel bits welded onto a frame.

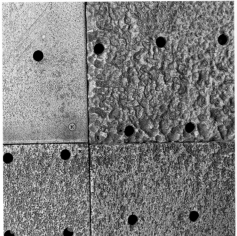

Stone Plaza

location: Ashino, Tochigi

architect: Kengo Kuma

date: 2000

This project, with a tea-ceremony room at the heart of it enclosed in an old stone warehouse, marked a turning point for the architect, Kengo Kuma. He is noted for his exploratory use of materials — old materials in new ways and new materials in traditional ways — and it was here at Stone Plaza in Tochigi Prefecture, completed in 2000, that he believes he first succeeded in creating an effective "weak" architecture. One of Kuma's aims in his work is to find a successor to the monumental solidity of much twentieth-century architecture, and this commission, from the owner of a stone company quarrying the local grey andesite, was a particular challenge. The client wanted to demonstrate new uses for the stone, and to show it as a material that could be soft and light. The site was originally used by the local rice association, and had several early twentieth-century stone warehouses. These were incorporated into the design, for which the architect invented two ways of making new buildings that were light, porous, and "transparent". One method involved the removal of every third stone "brick" from walls, the other developing new techniques with the client for cutting this volcanic stone into thin slices, which were then laid into "louvered" walls. It was agreed that the smallest of the old warehouses should be turned into a tea-ceremony room, which would also be experimental in its interior. Much of the effort went into lightening the dense, heavy sensation generated by the thick stone walls and lack of natural daylight. Accordingly, the floor for the tea-ceremony room was raised as a platform over gravel, with a gap between this and the walls.

108

Nestled between two new structures by the architect, the tea house was originally a small stone warehouse.

Concealed lighting under the platform helps to give an impression of it floating, while *shouji* screens along the side containing the doorway add softness and delicacy. Defining the space around the platform, Kuma made use of the new cutting technique to produce thin slats that he installed as light vertical pillars. These were treated by subjecting them to extremes of heat, which altered the colour (the precise hue depending on the temperature) and created extra texture as vesicles inside the stone bubbled outwards.

Left:
The solidity of the original stone is softened by the use of paper sliding *shouji* screens, *tatami* matting and wood, with thin vertical cuts of andesite.

Right:
Instead of a traditional *tokonoma* a modern scroll is simply hung on the stone wall. In the foreground is the *ro*, or sunken hearth, with a *chawan* (cup), *chasen* (whisk), and *chashaku* (scoop) laid out on a *fukusa* (silk cloth) in preparation for a tea ceremony.

Following pages:
Thinly sliced, then heat treated at different temperatures, the stone assumes different colours and textures. Vesicles extrude into surface bumps.

At the opposite end from the *kakejiku*, the sunken *ro* awaits guests. The preparation area is through the door at far left.

Uplighting was installed against the stone walls, below the raised platform supporting the *tatami* mats. A modern version of the *kakejiku* hangs on the unadorned wall.

Ichijuan

location: Mojiko Hotel, Mojiko, Fukuoka
architect: Shigeru Uchida
date: 1998

Built in 1998, this was one of the first tea-ceremony rooms created by the noted designer Shigeru Uchida. It was installed in the Mojiko Hotel, on the southern island of Kyushu, by architect Aldo Rossi, with whom Uchida has collaborated on other projects. Uchida began his continuing experimentation with tea-ceremony rooms here. "The main reason why I became interested in the tea room", he says, "is because I felt there was a great difference between the nature of space in the West and that of the East." One of the most transparent differences is the simplification of space, and as Uchida analyses it, "What characterises Japanese design of today is its endless pursuit of simplicity. Simplification is promoted by the belief that the true features of an object are revealed by simplification." In this room, frosted glass provides a modern interpretation of a floating void, the designer's re-creation of "the 'souan', the hut for the hermit who revered simplicity and who always had 'temporary housing' in mind, [and] was also a place of nothingness." A more subtle difference is that Japanese architecture incorporates many elements important to the shaping of consciousness. One of these is the pillar. *Chashitsu* feature a central pillar, or *nakabashira*, which creates an invisible division between the tea master (*teishu*) and others, and here Uchida makes it dominate the room. In Japan, the symbolic elements may be expressed by invisible "points" or by the relationship between objects. Uchida asserts that this vagueness is an extremely important feature of Japanese interior design.

Frosted glass walls bring a combination of vague light and shadows. Uchida identified with the master craftsman in Kyoto, Koji Fujii, who claimed that Japanese style is a delicate combination of space and the nature of the shadows created by it.

The minimalist glass cube sits on a concrete plinth. Rush *zabuton* (cushions) on the bench are for the waiting guests, and the *tsukubai* in the corner is for washing and purifying hands and mouth.

An adjacent, larger, tea-ceremony room is in more traditional style, save for the gently vaulted ceiling and white *tokonoma* with concealed lighting.

Niki Club

location: Nasu, Tochigi

designer/architect: Takashi Sugimoto
+ Akira Watanabe Architect & Associates

date: 1997

Interior designer Takashi Sugimoto, whose practice, Super Potato, has a long record of international hotel and retail projects, here in a secluded luxury resort in the hills of Tochigi Prefecture brought a sophisticated designer's eye to the *chashitsu* tradition. Niki Club, in a well-known summer resort area about an hour by fast train from Tokyo, was a collaboration between several architects and designers — a village-like complex intended as a Japanese interpretation of East meets West. As part of this design-conscious theme, Sugimoto introduced a structure of customised steel grilles. The walls are multi-layered, beginning with a standard steel lattice onto which have been welded a variety of cut steel plates for a complex textural effect. The final step was to burnish the metal by hand roughly using an angle grinder, bringing a handmade finish that is the industrial equivalent of wood shaved with a hand-axe (*naguri-shiage*) as seen at Shimakin (page 79).

Three of the eighteen rooms, each separate units within the hotel grounds, have their own tea-ceremony room attached.

On a winter's late afternoon, the metal grillework filters the sunlight to create a dappled chiaroscuro across the tea-ceremony utensils.

The grillework forms two walls and covers a low window. The scroll painting in the corner is by Arima Raitei, Chief Priest at the Golden Temple, or Kinkaku-ji, in Kyoto.

A fretwork skirting echoes the metal grille behind in a contrast of traditional and modern techniques.

Another view of the *chashitsu* bathed in light coming through the welded steel screens.

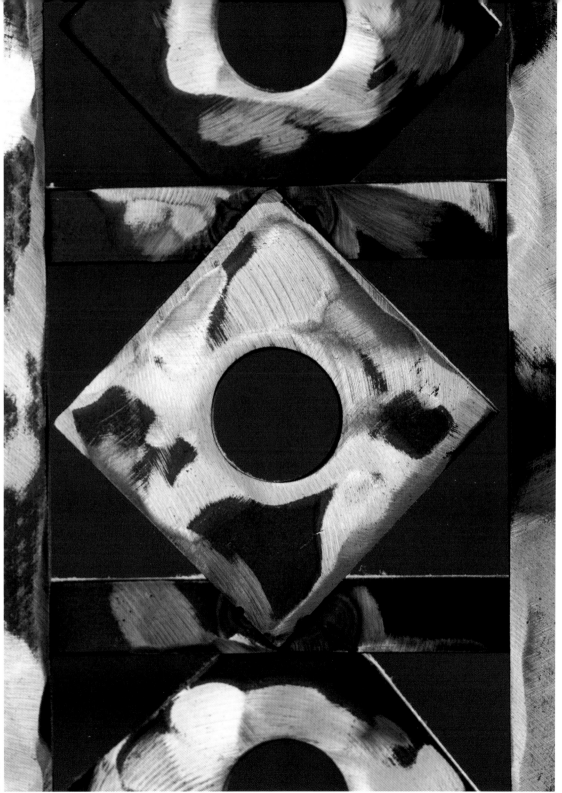

Cut steel shapes have been
welded onto a basic frame and
roughly burnished by hand.

Ujian (Existence of Time)

location: Hotel Laforet, Shinagawa, Tokyo

architect: Arata Isozaki,

built by Sotoji Nakamura

date: 1992

Gotenyama has for a long time been a favourite site for cherry blossom viewing in this expensive residential area of Tokyo. In this 1.6-acre garden, now in the grounds of a luxury hotel, an old tea house had fallen into disrepair. The owners came across drawings made in the 1980s by architect Arata Isozaki for a possible "nonfunctional" tea-ceremony room, and commissioned him to realise the plans on this site. Its most notable features are the introduction of new materials, including titanium, stainless steel, concrete, and etched glass, and the contrast between strong flat horizontal surfaces and curving, feminine verticals.

As in his most famous buildings, such as the Olympic Stadium in Barcelona and the Los Angeles Museum of Contemporary Art, Isozaki's design is characterised by bold forms and inventive detailing. His approach is based on the principle that, just as the tea ceremony itself depends on the arrangement of all the elements of the world of tea, so that "the entire affair depends on the guests and the circumstances of the moment", so the spaces of the tea house depend on "an aesthetic of composition and arrangement." Isozaki took this challenge to employ materials and forms not used in conventional tea spaces. This allowed him to expand the range of compositional freedom, although not without risk of failure by being unconventional.

The name given to the tea house, Uji, means the "existence of time", and is an idea taken from the renowned Zen Buddhist text *Shobogenzo* written by Dogen Zenji, the founder of the Soto Zen sect. In it, he wrote, "there is no space without time and temporal being which integrates time and space", referring to the time as conceived in terms of the deep significance of its own existence. Isozaki chose the name for his first tea house because for him the act of receiving tea "is like lending an ear to time". The words appear as calligraphy on the scroll in the *tokonoma* by Sobin Yamada, the head priest of Shinju-an, a subtemple of Daitoku-ji Temple in Kyoto.

The large, circular steel roof projects over the square, white concrete building, while a low etched-glass window transmits light through to the *ryureiseki* area.

The small entrance on the left is the *nijiriguchi*, while the full-sized doorway to the right is the entrance for the *ryureiseki* — the seated form of the tea ceremony.

The *honseki*, or main tea-ceremony room, seen from the *nijiriguchi* entrance, looking towards the *temae-za* (the space for making tea). The central pillar is a camellia from Tanba (*Tanba-tsubaki*), while the adjacent wooden panel is made from a hundred-year old cedar from Yakushima.

The area for the seated tea ceremony displays an eclectic mixture of modern materials and surfaces, including an undulating titanium wall, concrete floor, limestone wall, and stainless steel ceiling.

The *mizuya*, or service room for preparation, is partly visible from the outside through a window and cylinder in etched glass.

Garden Settings

Tetsu-no-chashitsu

location: Osaka

architect: Hiroaki Kimura,
Ks Architects

date: 2004

Right:
The re-modelled front entrance to
the preserved *minka* house.
Looming behind is a golf range.

Far right:
Folded steel sheeting gives
simplicity to the structure, sited
beyond a small pond in the garden.

The original house on this property in Osaka, of traditional single-storey *minka* farm-house design, was built in 1925, but was refurbished and extended by Hiroaki Kimura in 2004. To commemorate the tenth anniversary of the passing away of the architect's father, it was decided to build a tea-ceremony house that would be modern in form and materials, but traditional in its function and relationship to the old dwelling. Kimura chose to work in 9-mm sheet-steel, bent into shape at the factory, allowed to partially oxidise, and then sealed. The white roof is coated with an insulating emulsion containing four different ceramics to stabilise the temperature inside and counter the conductivity of the steel. It was located in the garden, so that it can be seen from the main residence over a low, wide Japanese-style veranda (*engawa*) and pond in the garden. The traditional Japanese appreciation of nature is fully staged in the blurred boundaries between inside and outside, bringing continuity of space to the household's everyday life.

The architect aimed for "a modern 'product-like' architecture rather than relying on pillars and beams like traditional Japanese architecture".

Seen from the living room,
across the veranda and garden,
the new tea house brings a
continuity of both space and
time to the dwelling.

The view from the tea house back
towards the old main building.

Jurinji-no-ie

location: Jurinji, Nara

architect: Yoshiji Takehara

date: 2000

Part of a complex, multi-level house near Osaka, in which the interconnecting spaces are as important as the rooms themselves, this *washitsu* by Osaka-based architect Yoshiji Takehara, looks out over a secluded, deep garden of bamboo. It is approached through twists and turns from the main entrance of the house, and this passage takes the form of a *roji* that draws inspiration from certain temples, in particular the Daitoku-ji Temple in Kyoto. Takehara, who declares his interest in what he calls the "architecture of ambiguous spaces", explains the importance of a circuitous approach and the surprise of the final destination: "What you first saw and expected as the scene that would greet you is changed through views that reveal themselves as you progress along the route, and this traditional method of design is what I try to incorporate in my residential houses." To link the *washitsu* more closely with this hidden courtyard, it is cantilevered so as to appear to float, and projects into the garden so that the sliding *shouji* screens can be opened up along two sides.

A small grove of thick-stemmed *mosodake* (Chinese) bamboo is planted outside the *washitsu*.

The view looking out from the *washitsu*, with the sliding *shouji* panels open.

Isolated from the rest of the house, the small room has its own courtyard.

Step House

location: Kuritani, Kanagawa

architect/designer: Ken Architects

+ Takeshi Nagasaki

date: 2005

The upper level entrance, in Western style, gives a view down to the *washitsu* and the iron plates, but reveals nothing of the secret garden underneath.

A bowl filled with rainwater on the corner of the main entrance steps that overlook the room and the iron plates covering the cave garden.

Left:
A special variety of sliding screen is *yukimi-shouji*, a two-layer vertically sliding window, in glass and Japanese paper. The lower section slides up for a view of the cave garden.

Below:
Symbolising the legendary Horai-san, the cave garden is connected with other fables of immortality, such as that of Urashima (the fisherman who is taken to an undersea palace but when he returns, homesick, finds that he has aged tremendously) and Sennin (the immortal spirit of an ascetic saint living in the mountains).

For this house a short distance south of Tokyo, the slope created certain restrictions, but also provided garden designer Takeshi Nagasaki with the opportunity to create a highly structured view from the *washitsu*, and this became the principal feature of the *tatami* room. The client's requirement was for a Western style view from the upper-level entrance, but a Japanese view from the *washitsu* on the lower level. The Japanese view proved the more demanding. In collaboration with the architect, Nagasaki organised the view from the room in such a way that the lower sections of the sliding *shouji* screens can be raised to reveal a compact garden-within-a-garden in the left corner. The steep slope was covered in grass to provide a relatively plain view overall, but was then cut into on the left to make a miniature landscape within a "cave" constructed of two overlapping sheets of oxidised iron projecting over stones. This exploits the Japanese love of shade (*inei*) and its ideological counterpart of *inyo*, which is the harmonised duality of light/shade and negative/positive (the Japanese reading of yin-yang). A flow of pebbles in front, running along the edge of the floor, represents the ocean. The symbolism of the ensemble is that of both a hermit's cave and Horai-san, an inaccessible island of eternal youth that regularly features in traditional Japanese gardens. Horai-san, sometimes translated as Treasure Island or Treasure Mountain, is an idyllic place borrowed from earlier Chinese myths.

The ceiling is constructed of stained planking spaced with black bamboo, with different thicknesses of bamboo attached below.

This special wall render is known as *warasusa-iri-tennen-tsutchikabe*, natural soil mixed with pieces of straw and old rope.

Modern half-length tatami mats known as *hanjou-tatami*. Normally, mats are arranged so that only three meet at a corner.

Yuishikian (Consciousness Only)

location: Akasaka, Tokyo

architect: Kisho Kurokawa

date: 2004

One of the most unusual locations for not just a tea house but a complete tea garden leading to it, is on the eleventh floor of a large apartment block in the heart of Akasaka, one of the best known entertainment and business districts of Tokyo. The owner, one of the country's most famous architects and a leading member of the Metabolist movement, is Kisho Kurokawa. The spacious terrace provided him with the opportunity, as he puts it, "to recreate a symbol that represents a formative, crucial, and yet forgotten model of Japanese aesthetics", and in so doing, enabled him to "enjoy a life in which the most advanced technology exists in symbiosis with tradition."

This garden is the descendant of two other gardens, the earlier of which goes back to the early seventeenth century. It was called Shosuitei and was at the Fushimi — the Kyoto residence of Enshu Kobori (1579–1647), a leading tea master who also served as construction minister under the first three Tokugawa shoguns. The tea aesthetic that Kobori promoted was known as *kirei-sabi*, or pretty rusticity. This tea-ceremony room was destroyed by fire, but its plan was recorded and it became the basis for another, in Takimotobo, a residence of Buddhist monks, constructed at the Iwashimizu Hashimangu shrine in Kyoto by the scholar-monk Shokado Shojo. Kurokawa spent seventeen years researching and building this contemporary tea house and its garden, and the reason he gives is "as a symbol of the aesthetic vision I call *hanasuki*". This invented term is Kurokawa's substitute for *wabisuki* (see Introduction), which he believes has become too narrowly interpreted as only spare and ascetic, and refers to an ambiguous, symbiotic aesthetic, which simultaneously embraces splendour and simplicity — and by extension also the contrast of modernity and tradition.

The garden begins at the door to the apartment, from where stepping stones lead to an outer passageway, a transitional space, and then to the inner *roji*, a garden of pines and shrubs that excludes all sense of the surrounding city. This leads, via a stone lantern and *tsukubai* water-basin for guests to wash their hands for symbolic purification, to the tea house itself.

Seen from the apartment entrance, the garden is a dense green island, completely unexpected in these surroundings.

A gate leads to an outer passageway (above, and in the lower right corner of the overhead view at left), an intermediate stage before entering the garden.

A *kutsunugi-ishi*, or stone for removing shoes, is the first step from the modern apartment to the garden.

By the outer gate, a bamboo mat weighted with a stone covers a water-basin.

Surrounded by a simple bamboo fence, the inner garden leads, by way of a water-basin, to the tea house, named Yuishikian after the central doctrine of the Hosso school of Buddhism, which holds that all existence is nothing but consciousness, and therefore there is nothing that lies outside the mind.

Mihara-no-ie

location: Mihara, Osaka

architect/designer: Chitoshi Kihara

+ Yasujirou Aoki

date: 1998

This dual use *chashitsu* and *washitsu* occupies one side of a small garden that is in many ways the visual centre of this house in Mihara, south of Osaka. Indeed, the configuration of the room and its sliding screens plays an important role in an orchestrated experience for the visitor. The first glimpse of both garden and tea-ceremony room is from the entrance path leading from the street, through an opening in the exterior wall. The next, full view of both is from the living room which, like the bulk of the accommodation in the house, is Western in style — its picture window reveals the wooden room and in the restrained gravel garden a single camellia of the type known in Japan as a white *wabisuke*. Finally, guests make their way to the tea-ceremony room, where the view is deliberately restricted. The arrangement on three levels of sliding panels, both solid and *shouji*, allows at best a fragmented view of the tree. The intention is to focus concentration, and guests must rely on their recent memory of the view from the living room — an afterimage of the tree and garden. In this way, architect Chitoshi Kihara and garden designer Yasujirou Aoki created a time sequence in the viewing of the garden, a sequence that accords with the formal progression of the tea ceremony. First a glimpse, then a complete view from the living room, and finally incompleteness, pushing the senses back onto accumulated experience. The tree outside the *chashitsu* was chosen for many reasons. It was this species that was supposed to have been brought back from a campaign in Korea by the Shogun Hideyoshi Toyotomi (1536–1598), patron of Sen no Rikyu (1522–1591), who perfected the tea ceremony. As a favourite of Sen no Rikyu, it was named with reference to the elusive Japanese concept of *wabi*, meaning rustic simplicity. But also, it is symbolic of medicine here in Japan and in China, and this is the houseowner's profession. Finally, the flowers do not fall petal by petal, but all at once, like a decapitation (*kubikiri*), and in this sense the camellia captures the samurai spirit.

The second view of the garden from the *washitsu*, deliberately partially obscured by the design of the sliding *shouji* and panels.

The view of the *washitsu* with its small curved-wall garden from the main living room's picture window.

The central pillar, or *nakabashira*, provides a focus for the geometrical division of the space.

The lower section of the back wall hinges open for ventilation.

Minamiazabu-no-ie

location: Minamiazabu, Tokyo
designer: Shunmyo Masuno
date: 2005

The traditional appearance of this exceptional suite of *chashitsu* and related spaces belies its very modern location and construction. Occupying one entire penthouse in a new luxury apartment building in fashionable Minamiazabu, close to Roppongi Hills, the interiors and garden were designed by Zen priest Shunmyo Masuno, well-known for his modern Zen gardens constructed around Japan and internationally. There were various restrictions, such as the concrete flooring, floor plan, and facilities for water supply and drainage, and the construction took two years. The result is a full-scale tea-ceremony room for samurai-style tea ceremony, in the Ueda school of tea. It includes a small partition room, salon, changing room, preparation area, waiting room, connecting corridor, and the tea-ceremony room itself. There are also three gardens: the small open space after the gate, the small (*tsubo-niwa*) garden in front of the salon, and the narrow garden in front of the waiting room.

Bamboo fencing encloses the garden in front of the salon to exclude the sense of the city all around. From a seated position inside, the sight lines are directed exclusively to the dry-stone garden by the position of the *shouji* screens.

Detail of the cross-tied bamboo, in which the fencing is horizontal and the supports vertical.

A partially cut stone, symbolising the stroke of a sword, in reference to the samurai style of the tea-ceremony room.

The garden in front of the waiting room shelter is named Seifu-tei, meaning "the garden of fresh wind". In contrast to the garden on the previous page, this is a space for walking in rather than looking at.

The salon is the largest room in the suite, facing out onto the austere, white Zen garden.

The reverse view through the
arched doorway from the
chashitsu to the corridor (above),
and the *chashitsu* itself (right).

The connecting corridor
leading from the garden,
waiting and preparation rooms
to the *chashitsu*, which is
reached through the small
archway at left

Following pages left:
The preparation room,
equipped with writing ledge.

Following pages right:
The small waiting area in front
of the *chashitsu*.

Ryogo-tei

location: Fujiidera, Osaka

garden designer: Masatoshi Takebe

date: 1995

Incorporated into one of the largest private gardens in the country, in Kansai, Ryogo-tei has one section that leads to a tea house in the style of the Mushanokojisenke — one of the three principal tea-ceremony schools. The modernity here, however, lies not in the tea house itself, but in the garden design, by Masatoshi Takebe. Well-versed in the many traditions of Japanese garden design, Takebe believes there are currently too many inferior imitations of tea gardens, or *chaniwa*, and that simply following traditional designs is no longer sufficient for a society that is changing so rapidly. Here, Takebe has created a fusion of English and Japanese styles, with an emphasis on bright colours that is now uncommon in Japan. Indeed, the entire garden contains more than 300 different species, including azaleas, peonies, and tulips. Close to the tea house are plantings of Japanese arums, including *Musashiabumi* and *Yukimochisou*, together with pink-flowering skullcap.

The entrance to the outer garden, with a winding stone path flanked by azaleas and rhododendrons.

A *tsukubai*, or stone water-basin, just inside the gate of the tea house garden, used for ritual washing by guests as they arrive.

A simple wooden porch-like structure, or *machiai*, where guests sit and wait to be called by the tea master.

The tea house, glimpsed through the foliage from the *machiai*.

Gallery-no-ie

location: Nara

architect/designer: Chitoshi Kihara +
Yasujirou Aoki

date: 2004

In another collaboration between architect Chitoshi
Kihara and garden designer Yasujirou Aoki — who
also created the *washitsu* with gardens on pages
44–49, 52–57, and 160–163 — aspect is crucial to the
success of this combined *washitsu* and *chashitsu*. A
gently winding path of stepping stones crosses white
gravel to the east entrance of the room, and the view back from here takes in the garden. These stones,
which include iron-brown *kurama-ishi* and black *maguro-ishi* from Kyoto, as well as *goshiki-jari* (five-
colour pebbles), form a *roji*, the traditional path to a tea-ceremony room. A more austere view faces north:
a long low window looking out onto plain raked gravel and a wall that re-creates, in a style called *bentiku-*

The east garden leading to the
washitsu. The stone bound with
rope, known as a *sekimori-ishi*,
signifies "do not enter" when
placed like this at the entrance.

The view from the *washitsu* onto the east garden.

bei – a 2,000 year-old Chinese technique involving tamping down many different clays. Inside, the large (*hachijou* or eight-tatami) *washitsu* has a *hon-juraku-nuri* earthen wall in the Kyoto style, the brownish earth originally from the Kyoto Nishijin area, that can also be seen in another *chashitsu*, Yokoo-tei, illustrated on pages 50–51.

The *tsukubai* to one side of the
path, for washing and purifying
hands and mouth.

The final stone of the path is
the *kutsunugi-ishi*, literally the
stone where shoes are
removed, and for this, Aoki
chose a *kurama-ishi* noted for
its iron-brown colour.

The north window of the room, with the *shouji* screens partly opened, and a *chigaidana* (literally "staggered shelves") of plate steel connected to two long shelves of cherry wood and glass.

A second entrance in the corner leads to the gallery of the house, which contains the owner's art collection. The garden wall at right is made from red clays, hemp fiber, gravels, and plaster in an ancient Chinese style.

A pattern of pine trees designed by Kihara and cut into the steel-plate *chigaidana* (staggered shelves) display. *Matsu* means not only "pine tree", but also "waiting for gods descending from heaven", and is a common visual theme.

The same pine tree motif carved on the *ranma*, or transom over the main partition in the room.

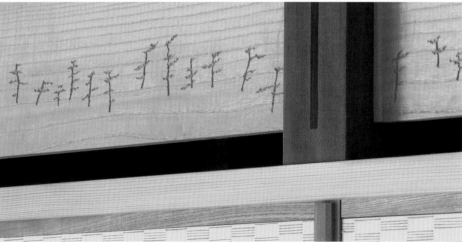

Contemporary
Interpretations

Souan (Simple Hut)

location: Yamagata
designer: Toshihiko Suzuki
date: 2003

In his mountainside atelier, Toshihiko Suzuki, professor at the Tohoku University of Art and Design, constructed this minimally cubic two-*tatami* tea-ceremony room. Working in his favourite material — aluminium — Suzuki had two aims. One was to play with the changing combinations of interior and exterior light, and the other was to blur the actual dimensions when sitting inside. Concealed interior tungsten lighting is computer-controlled, cycling up and down, while daylight filters through the circular holes cut out of the laminated, honeycomb aluminium walls. Feeling that aluminium would be too hard a finish for the interior, Suzuki had panels made by sandwiching the honeycomb centre in traditionally-made rice paper. The combination of panels and walls is 10 cm thick, and when the exterior light dominates guests inside feel the space is slightly larger than when the interior lights are stronger.

The designer's atelier, which houses the tea-ceremony room, on a mountain slope in Yamagata Prefecture.

A perfect cube of aluminium on the outside and rice-paper inside, Souan is a minimal blend of new and old materials.

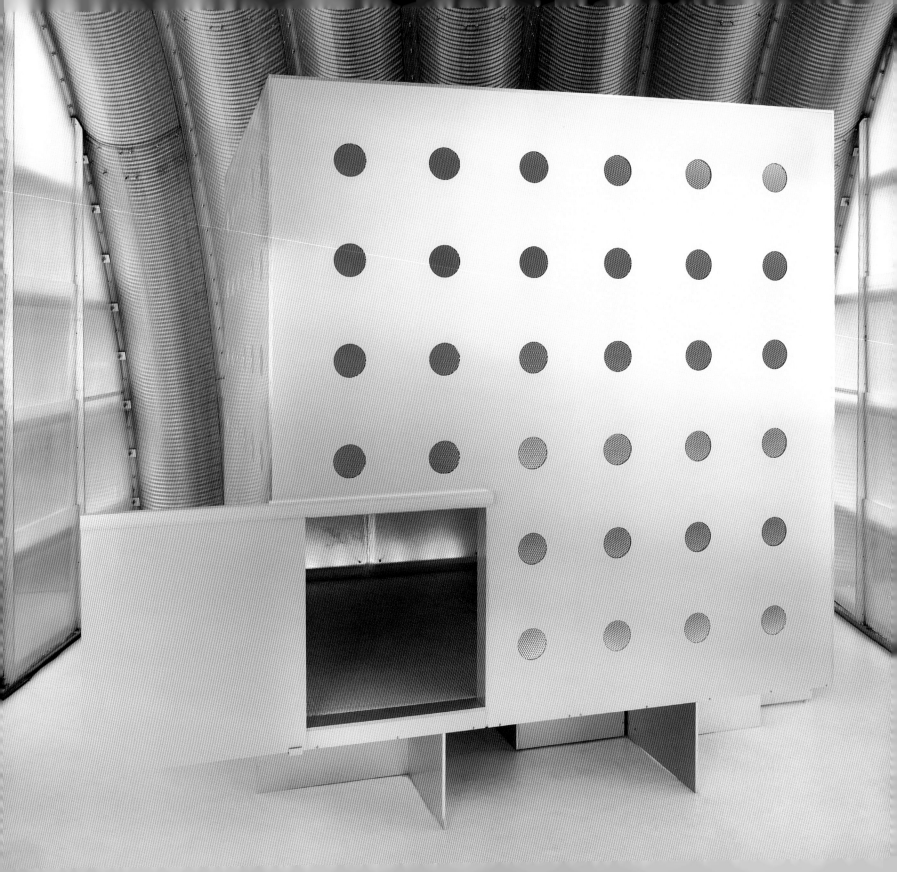

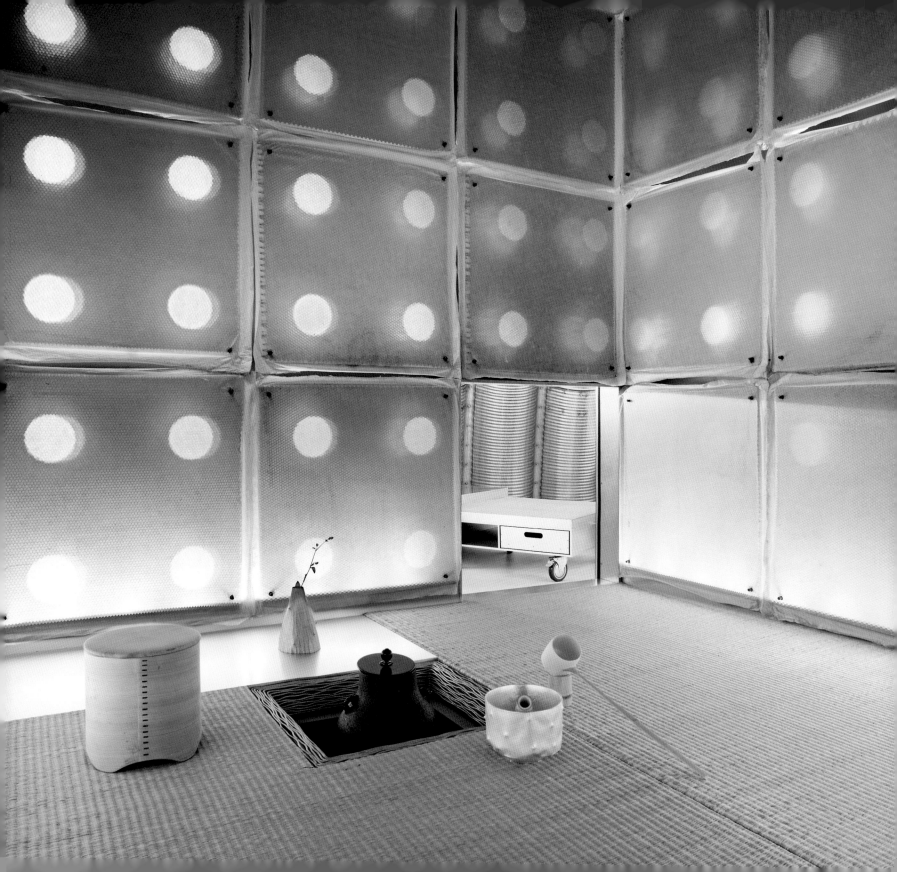

Left: A concealed lighting system cycles slowly from uplighting to downlighting and from dark to bright for a constantly changing effect. The circular holes in the aluminium laminate sandwich (detail opposite) also admit daylight.

Below: An old classic Airstream trailer in polished aluminium, imported from the United States, is used as an unusual *mizuya*, or kitchen preparation area.

Sankio (In the Mountains)

location: portable

designer: Shigeru Uchida

date: 2005

A modern scroll painting, *Uma* (Horse), by Keisuke Ngatomo hangs in the entrance vestibule.

Far right: With a floor area of 2.8 m² and a height of 2.3 m, the open structure of thin bamboo strips woven into a mesh is designed for portability.

The black painted mesh gives an ambiguous kind of transparency to the room and its contents.

The interior layout is non-traditional, with the hearth and utensils in one corner, while the *kakejiku* scroll and flower arrangement (on the right) are not placed in a recessed alcove.

Following pages left:
At a tea ceremony in the portable structure, the *teishu* (literally "house master") holds the bamboo ladle in a formal posture before preparing the water.

Following pages right:
The *kakejiku* scroll inside the room, entitled *Look*, is by Katsumi Asaba.

This cubic light structure is designer Shigeru Uchida's fifth in a series of portable *nijoudaime* (two and three-quarter mat) *chashitsu*, one of which is in the Conran Design Museum collection in London. Made of bamboo mesh supported by a frame of Japanese ash, and stained black, its essential characteristic is portability, which is key to the designer's concept of the inter-connection of interior and exterior space, and the relationship between man and nature. Like the previous designs, this is "moveable architecture" that straddles the border between "inside" and "outside" — interiors without walls that separate them from the exterior. According to art critic Ryu Niimi, "From the beginning, Uchida avoided strong, sturdy solids, and favoured the faint, transitory, and vulnerable. It might have been in defiance to the structural forms of modern Europe. He chose to pursue 'furniture with delicate lines'." Uchida himself says that "the vibration propagated by the sensibilities of the weak, fragmented, ephemeral, ambiguous, incomplete, and the like was indeed the vision of Japanese architecture. Sensibilities derived from the sitting down posture are sensitive to the natural vibrations such as the wind, sound, light, and so on. The sensation felt by quietly sitting down was to appreciate the delicate changes. An architecture that would enhance such sensations was not one of solid construction, but a fragile one that would be able to capture the 'sensory vibrations'". By constructing walls that are open and ephemeral — of woven bamboo strips — Uchida aims to enhance the ambiguity of sitting "inside" a structure yet fully open to the sounds and movements of "outside".

The *teishu* (above) and his
kimono-clad assistant (left)
conduct a series of tea
ceremonies at the first
presentation of the
chashitsu in a gallery in
Nishi-Azabu, Tokyo.

Kuan

location: Kyoto

architect: Terunobu Fujimori

date: 2004

This peculiar tea-ceremony room, with the name Kuan, is located in the back court of Tokyosho-ji, a small temple near the Shijo quarter of Kyoto. Formerly there was a toilet on the site, but it fell into disuse once a new flush lavatory was built inside the temple, and then was destroyed by the Hanshin earthquake in 1995. Terunobu Fujimori, who has designed many other tea-ceremony rooms, conceived the idea of a perched construction (he was at the time working his way towards the "tree house" on pages 230–235), with the practical benefit of damp protection. First, a chestnut tree was cut down from the chestnut forest near Fujimori's hometown and a section of the trunk with three forks was set into a concrete base to support the whole room. As with most of Fujimori's works, there is an intentional amateur component in the building, and most of construction and fittings were undertaken between April 2003 and May 2004 by the resident priest, Hitoshi Akino, following sketches drawn by Fujimori. The architect visited Kyoto once every one or two months to advise

A handmade window with irregularly leaded panes, designed by Fujimori, looks down on the small courtyard garden, with tea utensils in the foreground.

Stepping stones lead across a dry-stone garden from the living area of the temple, under a fanciful, moss-covered arch, to the small tea house in the far corner.

and supervise. The priest completed the building frame, stained-glass window, and even sheet copper roofing. A hand-built ladder, also in chestnut, provides access through the floor to the small, 3.6 m², room. Architect and client like to joke, "is this an opening for removing night soil, or an entrance to a tea room?" The small space seems more spacious than it is because of the large stained-glass sliding window facing the garden. On the white plaster wall, instead of a scroll picture, a painting is hung, the last work of the priest's mother, a well-known artist, Fuku Akino. Accompanying the painting, made on her trip to Africa, is a small bottle containing sand from the Western Sahara and her sketch book. This room does not have a fire pit, being designed not for the *chanoyu* tea ceremony as developed by Sen no Rikyu, but for the simpler *sencha-do* (boiled tea ritual). Thus, instead of whisking green powdered tea with hot boiling water from a fire pit, natural tea leaves are used. *Sencha-do* has attracted attention recently as a freer and less constrained tea ceremony than *chanoyu*, and is influenced by the ideas of Lao Tzu and Chuang Tzu.

The room laid out for *sencha-do*, the informal tea style.

Far left: The tea house is supported on the forks of an old chestnut tree. A ladder at right provides access through a floor hatch.

203

Koya

location: Millennium City,
near Narita, Chiba

architect: Hiroshi Iguchi, 5th World

date: 2003

One of several agricultural greenhouses set among thirty trees planted to give shade, the enclosure for Koya contains several other units, including a converted camper van partly visible by the entrance.

Set in open farmland near Narita Airport, four large greenhouses enclose an eco-village designed as both sustainable low-energy architecture and as a communal experiment. Within each greenhouse, surrounded by trees, are small raised dwelling units, most in wood. The project, called Millennium City, was realised by the formation of a non-profit organisation by the architect, and the members have a common interest in ecology and conservation. Most members use their small units at weekends, and there are no formal prescriptions for how they are utilised. This double structure was, at the suggestion of its co-owner, adapted by Iguchi to function when needed as a tea-ceremony room. Thus, there is a regular doorway, reached by ladder as with most of the units, but it also features a "crawling-in entrance" in the form of two low sliding doors and a connecting wooden tunnel to the neighbouring unit. The tea-ceremony area occupies two *tatami* mats of the entire double-unit space. The name comes from the term used at Millennium City for all of these small hut-like structures; *koya* is a general expression for all kinds of small living space, including dog kennels, and while as a name it sounds strange to Japanese ears, it was chosen to reflect the flexibility and lack of formal hierarchy at the commune.

Adapted from standard units in the communal development, the raised rooms stand in one corner of the large greenhouse.

One end of the raised *chashitsu*, with the *nijiriguchi*, or crawling-in entrance, on the left. Behind the hearth are two small sliding doors that lead to another unit that functions as the *mizuya*.

Following pages left:
The minimal, geometric view from the hearth and entrance.

Following pages right:
The box construction of the unit, with diagonal braces, is in Japanese cedar. Translucent acrylic panels bring an enveloping, diffused light from the outside.

Kian

location: Okinawa

designer/architect: Amon Miyamoto
+ Tetsuo Goto

year: 2000

Despite its modern and highly unusual appearance, this tea-ceremony room named Kian, on the southern island of Okinawa, embodies some of the most traditional principles. Built in 2000 as part of the Asian Gate House, owned by the theatre and film director Amon Miyamoto, Kian's bare concrete finish frames an innovative interpretation of the *tokonoma* and *kakejiku* — the alcove and scroll painting — in the form of a red lacquered ledge and a thin vertical window looking out onto a highly controlled view of the Okinawan coastline. This view is, in fact, the chief inspiration for the entire house. Okinawa suffers particularly from typhoons, which have contributed to the distinctive erosion of its coast. The flat bedding of the rock here has produced a low cliff, into which the house was built, looking out over a very wide and shallow bay, scattered with huge boulders. Nowadays, most Okinawans prefer to build their houses away from the coast for safety and convenience, but Miyamoto decided to build in an exposed position, and utilise the rock formations. With Takamatsu-based architect Tetsuo Goto, he designed the house — and its tea-ceremony room — to "borrow" the landscape beyond in the old concept of *shakkei*, or borrowed landscape. One of the visual principles of the tea ceremony is restriction of view, yet as a child Miyamoto had an innocent urge to see more, and later decided to realise his ambition to create a tea-ceremony room with a window. To him, it relates to the experience of a priest opening and closing a sliding door to reveal briefly a view beyond. Careful siting of the house gives controlled views of the rock and bay from different rooms, and here it creates an inspired, real-life version of a scroll painting in the mountain-water Chinese style: the side of the rock falling into the composition from the left. The ledge in front, coated in red lacquer with a single shallow circular depression, is minimal in form, but its inspiration is the priest's desk for *shakyo* — the copying of Buddhist sutras. Only later did this become the more decorative, less functional *tokonoma*. The flower arrangement is here always a single bloom floating in the water-filled depression.

The siting of the house and the long vertical window of the *chashitsu* take in one falling edge of the rock. Combined with sea and sky, this makes a living scroll painting in the mountain-water tradition.

Seen from the shore at low tide, the rock selected to be a part of the carefully composed view is actually similar in size to the house itself.

M House

location: Shinagawa, Tokyo

architect: Ken Yokogawa

date: 2005

The *chashitsu* occupies the upper part of this projection, and is reached from a rooftop terrace.

Far right: The *tokonoma* alcove, with a low, brushed aluminium ledge, receives raking light from the side.

A suspended cupboard in one
corner is used for the storage
of futons — the *chashitsu*
doubles as a simple *tatami*
room for guests.

Detail of the floating wall and
ceiling panels — pegboard pasted
over with handmade paper.

Following pages left:
Detail of the earthen mud-
plaster finish on the wall
behind the *tokonoma*.

Following pages right:
A major feature of the room is
the diffusion of daylight from
the glass wall and ceiling,
using perforated pegboard on a
floating panel.

As part of a new house built in Shinagawa for a young professional couple, architect Ken Yokogawa, whose modern temple *chashitsu* appears on pages 88–99, was given the brief to incorporate an informal tea-ceremony room using new materials and new design ideas, while still respecting the traditions of the Way of Tea. He located it on the upper floor, in a projecting wing that allows two large-area sources of light, from a glass wall and ceiling, which he then diffused with panels of pegboard covered with *Tosa-washi*, a highly regarded kind of handmade Japanese paper from Tosa, in Shikoku. The wall panel against the window floats so that, in addition to the soft illumination coming through the perforated board with its natural coloured paper covering, daylight also seeps strongly around the edges, highlighting the contrasting textures of aluminium, earthen plaster, and *tatami*.

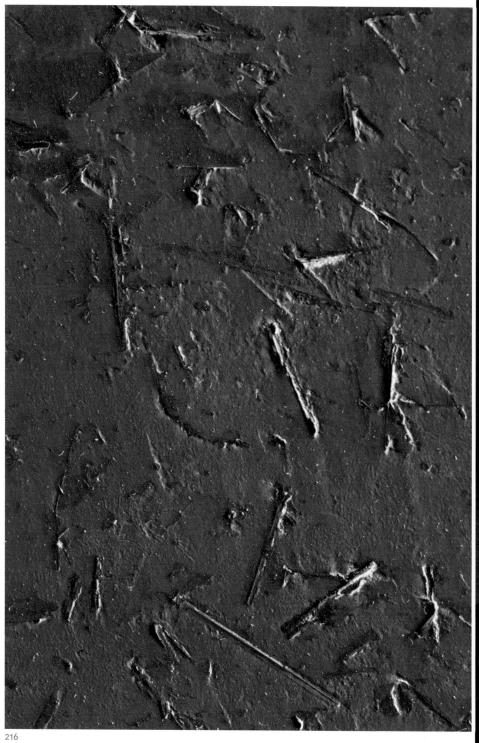

The *mizuya*, or preparation area, adjacent to the *chashitsu*.

Ladles and a cleaning brush hang
in the *mizuya* next to the tap.

Sakuragaoka-no-ie

location: Tama, Tokyo

architect: Kunihiko Hayakawa

date: 1994

For a house in Sakuragaoka, west of Tokyo, architect Kunihiko Hayakawa created a tea-ceremony room as what he calls an "apparatus", embedding a cylinder into the structure. The tea-ceremony room occupies the upper part and faces inwards through a small window onto a roof terrace, while the lower half of the cylinder houses a kitchen and entertainment system. Hayakawa designed the room in primary colours — blue walls with red and yellow fittings. In place of the *tokonoma* there is simply a polished metal floor section, perforated metal light and a small ceramic vase. Access is in the form of a marine tubular steel ladder, 55 cm in width, which can be raised and lowered by means of a wire block pulley. This adds both to the formal restrictions of entering a tea-ceremony room through the *nijiriguchi* and to the privacy (with the ladder raised, the room becomes completely isolated). A small window gives out onto a roof terrace fitted to function as the *mizuya*, or kitchen area, for washing the various utensils and supplies, and boiling the water.

The street entrance to the house. The circular top of the *chashitsu* rises above the cubic structure of this wing.

Far right: The interior of the circular space, in primary colours, looking towards the *nijiriguchi*.

The *mizuya*, or preparation area,
is converted from part of the roof
terrace. The two glass panels
forming part of the low wall rotate
on hinges to form a low table.

Looking down from the
nijiriguchi, with the
counter-balance ladder
in raised position.

Fujimian (Mount Fuji View)

location: Kofu, Yamanashi

architect: Atsushi Kitagawara

date: 1994

Located on the roof of a commercial building within sight of Mount Fuji (on clear days), this tea-ceremony room is positioned to make use of the view of the mountain, as its name implies. It is designed to give a floating impression, while the interior makes deliberate use of a mixture of traditional and modern materials. The roof, covered with copper that has been allowed to weather naturally to green, has a *mukuri* curve (a traditional form in Japanese architecture, part of a parabola with an inclined axis) to give a sensation of lightness and leaning to the structure. Interior floor and walls are also built so as to appear to "float". The architect made deliberate use of industrial materials, including aluminium pipes, in combination with wood, earth, and *tatami* as a way of stressing the long tradition of pre-fabrication in Japanese tea-house architecture. The dimensions are in the *sanjoukoma* tradition (*sanjou* means three tatami mats and *koma* is an architectural term describing a small-sized tea-ceremony room).

Tesuki-washi, handmade paper, printed with a diamond pattern.

Right: The tea house on the roof terrace is approached by a walkway crossing white pebbles.

A loose grille of parallel aluminium tubes forms a floating ceiling.

A wooden arch sits over one end of the room, with its raised floor.

Left: The reverse view from under the wooden arch. The *ro*, in the middle of the floor, is covered for the summer.

Right: The *tokonoma* recess, with an elegantly curved *tokobashira*, or alcove pillar.

Takasugian (Too High)

location: Chino, Nagano
architect: Terunobu Fujimori
date: 2004

Completed in June 2004, Takasugian is one of architect Terunobu Fujimori's most widely known works. A tea-ceremony room perched among the trees in his native Chino in Nagano Prefecture, swaying perceptibly in the wind, this "hideout in the treetops", as he envisioned it when planning began in 2000, is among the quirkiest constructions from an architect who follows very much his own path. Fujimori, who designed the tea-ceremony rooms on pages 58–61 and 200–203, is also Professor of Architectural History at Tokyo University, and is a self-professed "architectural detective", scouring Japan and the world for hidden vernacular structures. Takasugian follows his invented canon of naive architecture that celebrates natural materials — in particular, plants, wood, earth, and stone. The name given by Fujimori means approximately "the too-high tea room"; it is 10 m from the ground to the top of the roof. Access is through very much of a "crawling-in entrance", a small opening in the floor at the top of a 6-m ladder. Strictly speaking, this is not a tree house because it was not built on a living tree, but on the trunks of two chestnut trees felled from a nearby common forest. Each is about 30 cm in diameter and 8 m in length, buried to a depth of 1.5 m and set in concrete. The total floor area is 6.24 m². Construction began in October 2003, as usual as a collaboration between postgraduate students and the Jomon Kenchiku-dan (Jomon Culture Construction Company) — a group of Fujimori's friends who share his architectural interests. The design was continually adapted to the site during construction, which in addition to the chestnut trunks includes plastered Japanese cedar plywood and roof sheathing of hand-beaten copper plates. Small windows open on three sides, while a hearth and chimney in one corner are for boiling water for the tea ceremony. Osamu Ishiyama, architect and professor at Waseda University in Tokyo, calls it, "a misfit outside any conventional category, so 'out of it' that it's interestingly Bohemian," and sees a wider symbolism: "It sort of floats out there, a perfect match with current Japan, a country that skipped maturity and slipped right into its twilight days. Only Fujimori, the ultimate amateur who abhors sophistication, could do it."

Rising through the trees, the
"too-high tea-room" is by any
definition one of the most
unusual *chashitsu* ever
constructed, and has attracted
wide attention throughout Japan.

231

Hand-beaten small copper sheets
clad the chimney and roof.

The sparse interior looks out
through a low-set window onto
the surrounding hills.

A small section of one of the
chestnut trunks protrudes
through the white plastered
wall. A simple hearth occupies
one corner, with the chimney
flue directly above it.

In another quirky touch, a small skylight recessed into the apex of the roof is lined with burnished gold leaf.

Nijou

location: portable
designer: Toshihiko Suzuki
date: 2006

A development of an earlier design that functioned, less specifically, as a meditative space, Nijou (a measurement of area meaning "two-*tatami* space") was created by designer Toshihiko Suzuki as a portable tea-ceremony room, completely functional for one tea master and one guest. Suzuki's fascination with aluminium led him to the idea of a large case that would unfold to reveal two *tatami* mats in traditional *igusa* straw — combining modern industrial methods with the traditional. Ultimate weight reduction was needed for portability, and the structure chosen was 10 mm-thick aluminium honeycomb — two solid sheets sandwiching the honeycomb core, producing the strongest panel structure with the lightest weight. A complex structural arrangement of aluminium tubes and elasticated shock cords is then erected to support four triangular sails that act as a light ceiling. This superstructure is based on Buckminster Fuller's "tensegrity" principle, in which tension is used primarily and compression secondarily. A gas-fuelled cooker for heating the water used in the ceremony fits into the base. Nijou is part of the designer's continuing exploration of the connection and tension between products and space.

When packed, Nijou resembles an over-sized aluminium briefcase. It hinges open to become two joined *tatami* mats, with a built-in *ro*, and the covering is assembled by hooking the shock cords sheathed in aluminium tubes to eyelets around the edge.

Acknowledgements

My sincere thanks to all the owners of the *chashitsu* included in this book, the majority of whom prefer not to be named, for reasons of privacy. It was a special privilege to be allowed to intrude on these very particular and private spaces. Thanks also to Noriko Sakai, who arranged most of the visits and who accompanied me, and without whom this book would not have been possible.

The publishers would like to thank the following people for their help and support on this book:
Andrea Albertini of Damiani Editore, Jonathan Earl of Thames & Hudson, Henry Russell, Sue Farr, Chizuko Takagi, and Jessie Mlinaric.